CONTENTS

PART ONE

INTRODUCTION

HOW TO STUDY A POEM

Studying on your own requires self-discipline and a carefully thought-out work plan in order to be effective.

- Poetry is the most challenging kind of literary writing. In your first reading you may well not understand what the poem is about. Don't jump too swiftly to any conclusions about the poem's meaning.
- Read the poem many times, and including out loud. After the second or third reading, write down any features you find interesting or unusual.
- What is the poem's tone of voice? What is the poem's mood?
- Does the poem have an argument? Is it descriptive?
- Is the poet writing in his or her own voice? Might he or she be using a persona or mask?
- Is there anything special about the kind of language the poet has chosen? Which words stand out? Why?
- What elements are repeated? Consider alliteration, assonance, rhyme, rhythm, metaphor and ideas.
- What might the poem's images suggest or symbolise?
- What might be significant about the way the poem is arranged in lines? Is there a regular pattern of lines? Does the grammar coincide with the ending of the lines or does it 'run over'? What is the effect of this?
- Do not consider the poem in isolation. Can you compare and contrast the poem with any other work by the same poet or with any other poem that deals with the same theme?
- What do you think the poem is about?
- Every argument you make about the poem must be backed up with details and quotations that explore its language and organisation.
- Always express your ideas in your own words.

This York Note offers an introduction to the poetry of W.B. Yeats and cannot substitute for close reading of the text and the study of secondary sources.

W.B. Yeats (1865–1939), the twentieth-century's outstanding poet, wrote some of his finest idealistically romantic poetry over 100 years ago, in the nineteenth century. In his twenties and thirties he created the **genre** of **Celtic Twilight** poetry, drawing upon local traditions and Gaelic mythology as well as his knowledge of mysticism, magic and the occult: all new subject matter for most of his readers.

In somewhat disillusioned middle age, occupied with the struggle to create and maintain an Irish national theatre, he strengthened his poetry, stripping it of its decorative elements, even writing polemical poems on public events. During the last twenty-two of his seventy-three years, however, his poetry blossomed into new life, private and public themes blending in magnificently evocative poems. These were questioning, declarative, commemorative, prophetic, arresting, modern. His style changed, in diction, **imagery**, poetic techniques, as he strove constantly and successfully to develop his craft, his command of words, his complete commitment to poetic integrity.

> Things fall apart; the centre cannot hold;
> Mere anarchy is loosed upon the world,
> The blood-dimmed tide is loosed, and everywhere
> The ceremony of innocence is drowned;
> The best lack all conviction, while the worst
> Are full of passionate intensity. ('The Second Coming')

He wrote poems which recognise and record the effect of political martyrdom, for Yeats realised that the leaders of the Irish Rising of Easter 1916 who were executed by firing squads had become 'Transformed utterly: / A terrible beauty is born' ('Easter 1916').

In poems recording events after that Rising he laments the decline from the false confidence of the Edwardian peace, that things were gradually improving. Now the days seem to him to have become dragon-ridden. He faces the situation bleakly:

> But is there any comfort to be found?
> Man is in love and loves what vanishes,
> What more is there to say? ('Nineteen Hundred and Nineteen')

Yeats saw the decline and fall of great houses in Ireland; he records the chaos and helplessness that civil war creates:

> We are closed in, and the key is turned
> On our uncertainty; somewhere
> A man is killed, or a house burned,
> Yet no clear fact to be discerned. ('Meditations on Time of Civil War')

Other poems seize upon moments of crisis in the history of civilisation, stark in their realisation of destruction and their awareness of how 'conduct and work grow coarse, and coarse the soul.' Nonetheless, they bravely recognise man's capacity for regeneration:

> All things fall and are built again,
> And those that build them again are gay. ('Lapis Lazuli')

Yeats wrote some of this century's finest **elegies**: poems lamenting Major Robert Gregory, a gifted man with a Renaissance-like spread of interests and accomplishments who met his death as a wartime pilot; 'All Souls' Night', an atmospheric poem celebrating three eccentric friends of his youth; and 'The Municipal Gallery Revisited' with its dignified praise of his collaborators in the creation of the Abbey Theatre, Lady Gregory and Synge. Two poems about Lady Gregory, 'Coole Park, 1929' and 'Coole Park and Ballylee, 1931', pay memorable tribute to her achievement. In the same way 'Beautiful Lofty Things' selects dramatic moments in the lives of others, imbuing them with concentrated, vibrant poetic expression.

The sheer range and variety of Yeats's poetry is impressive: from the early delicate, idealistic poems of romantic devotion such as 'The Cloths of Heaven' to the vigorously insistent physical emphasis of the later sensuality of the Crazy Jane poems; from tributes to Irish revolutionary leaders such as Edward Fitzgerald, Wolfe Tone, Robert Emmet, Charles Stewart Parnell and John O'Leary (a list he had to extend by the addition of the leaders of the 1916 Rising and, later, Kevin O'Higgins) to the discovery in middle age of the significance of the eighteenth-century Anglo-Irish writers who displayed a spirit of free enquiry and independent thought, Swift, Berkeley, Goldsmith and Burke; from spontaneous, economically compacted poems such as 'The Wheel', its eight lines suggesting that nature and human life are part of a cyclical pattern, or 'The Four Ages of Man', an eight-line, compressed, **metaphysical** description of the four ages of individual man and the four ages of civilisation, to the longer meditative poems, such as 'The Tower' and 'A Dialogue of Self and Soul' and meditative poems, such as 'Among Schoolchildren'.

Many poems express Yeats's hatred of the infirmities of old age, many strike brave attitudes in the face of oncoming decrepitude and death. 'The Man and the Echo', set in the Sligo countryside he had always loved, a dramatically intense poem, written near the end of his own life, faces the ultimate reality: he cannot answer his own questioning about what happens after life. He realises that his knowledge must indeed be limited to the 'here and now'.

Yeats's poems are often very closely interrelated: youthful themes re-emerge but, reinforced by experience, he rediscovers them with fresh, renewed excitement. 'I have spent my life saying the same thing in different ways', he told his wife. And he rewrote his poems frequently:

> The friends that have it I do wrong
> When ever I remake a song
> Should know what issue is at stake:
> It is myself that I remake. (Untitled)

So rewritten poems are often very different from their early versions (and occasionally can cause confusion because they were sometimes included in their altered form in later editions of early volumes along with early poems in their early versions). When he was young his Muse, he remarked, was old, but as he grew older his Muse grew younger. Zest and intensity inform poems about the mask, the creative tensions between the self and anti-self, and the pull of the extremities between which, he thought, man runs his course.

Like many great poets Yeats also wrote fine thoughtful prose: autobiographies, essays and introductions, notes and reviews, short stories, radio talks and Senate speeches. There are literally thousands of his letters extant. His sense of the dramatic was not confined to his plays but irradiates his prose as well as his poetry, but while his plays often concentrate upon a moment of crisis which illuminates a character's personality they also exhibit the forcefulness of his highly original imagination: he could display a strange sense of comedy, as in *The Player Queen*, or exhibit a convincing conversational realism, as in *The Words Upon the Window-Pane*.

One of the most striking aspects of his work is his ability to draw upon very disparate material – Homer jostles with the occult, Gaelic myth with English romanticism, his philosophical and historical reading with his own critical attitudes to modern life. But the repeated connections, between poem and poem, symbol and symbol, image and image, are there: they interlock; meanings become clarified and expanded the more that readers know the poetry, as indeed Yeats expected them to. He wanted his poems to have the immediacy of speech, but of an ordered speech. He was delighted by an American critic who praised his language as public. He wrote for the ear (often chanting his verses aloud to himself, over and over again as he composed them). His poetry is at its best when read aloud, for a powerful, effective **rhetoric** controls and shapes it. Yeats's thought and emotional force, welded together through his technical skill, seek, indeed demand his hearers' full attention. He repays them with ideas, imagery and phrases that, once assimilated, cannot easily be forgotten or ignored. His is, quite simply, powerfully evocative poetry dealing with large concepts at once contradictory and yet consistent. He gives us, in all its blending of the individual and the general, real and imagined both, a truly impressive vision of human existence.

PART TWO

COMMENTARIES

This York Note is based on W.B. Yeats: *Selected Poetry*, ed. A. Norman Jeffares (Macmillan, 1999), containing 177 poems, which is itself based upon *Collected Poems* (1950) and includes all the poems mentioned in this Note, except for 'Adam's Curse'. There is a Penguin edition, *Selected Poetry*, ed. Timothy Webb (Penguin Poetry Library, 1991) which contains 180 poems with early versions of some, and is based with various exceptions on *Collected Poems* (1933) up to *The Winding Stair*, after which the editor has chosen texts from individual volumes, though for *Last Poems* he has gone to various sources. This Penguin edition, however, does not include the nineteen poems marked with an asterisk (*), but does contain 'Adam's Curse'. Both selections have introductions and notes.

There is a good deal of argument about the final arrangement of Yeats's poems. The *Collected Poems* (1933, expanded in 1950 by poems written from 1933 to 1939) was published for a popular market and at the publisher's suggestion the longer poems were placed at the end of the volume in a section called 'Narrative and Dramatic'. A two-volume posthumous edition, *The Poems of W.B. Yeats* (1949), had the poems arranged chronologically as Yeats preferred; the last section follows the order he prepared before his death.

For current editions of the *Collected Poems* in print, see Further Reading.

Figures without brackets given after the poem's title refer to its date of writing; bracketed figures to its first publication date.

from CROSSWAYS (1889)

This heading was first used for a group of poems in *Poems* (1895), most of them taken from *The Wanderings of Oisin* (1889). The poems were written when Yeats was trying 'many pathways'.

THE STOLEN CHILD   (1886)

A child is lured from this tragic world into the idyllic land of faery

Yeats is moving away from the Indian and Arcadian poems with which he began writing, such as 'The Song of the Happy Shepherd', 'The Sad Shepherd', 'Anashuya and Vijaya', 'The Indian upon God' and 'The Indian to his Love' (see *Collected Poems*, *The Poems. A New Edition* and *Yeats's Poems*) to Irish material. This poem is set in Sligo, the names of places locating it firmly there. And it reflects Yeats's interest in the belief in the supernatural that he found among the people in the west of Ireland, in particular the idea that the fairies carried off children from the human world. The poem is not so much escape from the 'real' world as escape into fairyland. Yeats called it not 'the poetry of insight and knowledge' that he hoped to write but poetry of 'longing and complaint'.

Sleuth Wood (Irish: *sliu*, a slope) Yeats alludes to this wood elsewhere by its more usual name Slish Wood (Irish: *slios*, inclined); it runs along the lower slopes of the Killery mountains at the edge of Lough Gill, County Sligo
Rosses a seaside village about five miles from Sligo, where the Yeats family spent summer holidays with Pollexfen and Middleton cousins. Yeats described Further Rosses midway between Knocknarea and Ben Bulben as 'a very noted fairy locality' in a note on the poem, and in *Mythologies*, (pp. 88–9), described a corner of it as being a place where the Sidhe or fairies might carry off a man's soul if he fell asleep there
Glen-Car (Glen of the Standing Stone) with several waterfalls, between Ben Bulben and Cope's Mountain, County Sligo

from THE ROSE   (1893)

The Rose was a heading first used by Yeats in *Poems* (1895) for a group of shorter poems, included earlier in his *The Countess Kathleen and Various Legends and Lyrics* (1892). The Rose had various **symbolic** meanings; as a title it probably means the 'Eternal Rose of Beauty and of Peace'. It also was used in the ordinary sense of a rose (as flower, plant or tree) in love poetry, and Yeats knew Irish poets had used it to symbolise Ireland (as in the 'little black rose' of Aubrey De Vere (1814–1902), or the 'Dark Rosaleen' of James Clarence Mangan). It was also used to symbolise the Rose of Friday in Irish poetry. Yeats's membership of the Order of the Golden Dawn gave him other symbolic meanings for the rose. In Rosicrucian symbolism the four leaves of the Rose and the Cross make a mystic marriage, the rose feminine, the cross masculine; the rose blooms on the sacrifice of the cross. So the Rose symbolised spiritual beauty, and love, and Ireland, and intellectual beauty – and Maud Gonne, with whom he had fallen in love in 1889.

FERGUS AND THE DRUID   (1892)

Disillusioned, King Fergus seeks a druid's 'dreaming wisdom'

This poem, later extensively revised, deals with Fergus MacRoy (or MacRoigh), a legendary king of Ulster, who married Ness (or Nessa). She persuaded him to allow her son by a previous marriage, Conor MacNessa, to rule for a year in his stead, and effectively tricked him out of his kingdom at the end of the year. Yeats found his material in Sir Samuel Ferguson's (1810–86) poem 'The Abdication of Fergus MacRoy'. Fergus lived out his days hunting, fighting and feasting. He was a poet and in the Irish saga, the *Tain bo Cuailgne*, he was the lover of Maeve, Queen of Connaught.

shape to shape   shape-changing is a feature of Irish mythology

Druid   druids were priests, prophets, wise men and magicians

Red Branch kings   the Red Branch heroes who served Conchubar (or Conor – Yeats also used Conhor, Concobar and Concubar), the king of Ulster; they lived at Emain Macha (Irish: the Twins of Macha, who was an Irish horse goddess), his capital near modern Armagh

subtle Conchubar   the adjective conveys something of the king's character, which emerged in the tale of 'The Fate of the Children of Usna'. He wanted to marry Deirdre, a young girl who was the daughter of Felimid, his harper. She was hidden away in the hills in the charge of an old nurse, Lavarcham, but fell in love with Naoise, one of the Red Branch heroes. They ran away to

Scotland with Naoise's brothers Ainle and Ardan, the other children of
Usna. Fergus was sent as a guarantor of safe conduct to bring them back,
Conchubar having promised there would be no reprisals. Fergus, however,
was under *geasa* (Irish = taboo) never to refuse an invitation to a feast, and
Conchubar arranged that Barach, another Red Branch hero, should invite
him to one, and in his absence the children of Usna were killed
treacherously by Conchubar

quern apparatus for grinding corn, usually made of two circular stones, the
upper one turned by hand

slate-coloured thing the bag of dreams

CUCHULAIN'S FIGHT WITH THE SEA   (1892)

The death of Cuchulain

This poem, later extensively revised, deals with the death of
Cuchulain (Yeats also spelled the name as Cuhoollin and
Cuchullin; he pronounced it Cuhoolin. It should, however, be
pronounced Cu-hullin). His name (Cu Culann) means the Hound
of Culann; he was sometimes called the Hound of Ulster. The
name was given to him by Cathbad the Druid because, having made
his way to Conchubar's court at the age of seven, he killed the fierce
hound of Culann (or Culain) the smith in self-defence, and said
that in compensation he would undertake its work of protecting the
smith's flocks and other possessions. He was originally called
Setanta, and was the son of Sualtim and Dechtire (Conchubar's
sister). In the tales he is the greatest of the heroes of the Red
Branch, famous for his fighting ability and prodigious strength.

Emer Cuchulain's wife, Emer of Borda, the daughter of Forgael. His wooing
of her is told in *The Book of the Dun Cow*. Yeats derived this poem from
oral tradition, a ninth-century tale in 'The Yellow Book of Lecan' and
Jeremiah Curtin's *Myths and Folklore of Ireland* (1890). In 'The Yellow
Book of Lecan' version Cuchulain's son is called Conlaech, and his mother
is Aoife, with whom Cuchulain had an affair when he was in Scotland being
trained in fighting by Scathach, an Amazon. Yeats may have confused Emer
and Aoife

dun a fort

raddling ... raddled reddening with dye, reddened
the web woven stuff
cars of battle chariots
one sweet-throated Eithne Inguba, Cuchulain's young mistress
herd herdsman, in charge of cattle
Red Branch see notes on 'Fergus and the Druid'
young sweetheart Eithne Inguba
Conchubar see notes on 'Fergus and the Druid'
sweet-throated maid Eithne Inguba
Druids see notes on 'Fergus and the Druid'
the horses of the sea the waves

THE LAKE ISLE OF INNISFREE   (1890)
(See Extended Commentaries – Text 1)

THE SORROW OF LOVE   (1892)

A woman arouses man's sorrow, while the natural world continues, indifferent and relentless

One of the best-known examples of Yeats's rewriting of his early
work. Compare, for instance, with the first **stanza** of the early
published version:

The quarrel of the sparrows in the eaves,
The full round moon and the star-laden sky,
And the loud song of the ever-singing leaves
Had hid away earth's old and weary cry.

The MS described the moon as 'withered'; in the next line the 'loud
chaunting' of the leaves is characterised as 'wearisome'

a girl presumably Helen of Troy, though the poem also relates to Maud
Gonne
Odysseus Homer's *Odyssey* tells how Odysseus, son of Laertes, King of the
island of Ithaca, having taken part in the Greeks' expedition to Troy (which
they besieged for ten years before taking it through the stratagem of the
wooden horse) spent ten years returning home
Priam Homer's *Iliad* tells how Priam, King of Troy, was killed after the fall
of Troy by Neoptolemus, son of the Greek warrior Achilles. Priam's children

included Paris (who caused the Graeco-Trojan war by bringing back to Troy
with him Helen, the wife of Menelaus, King of Sparta); Hector (killed by
Achilles); and Cassandra (captured after the fall of Troy and brought to
Argos as a slave or concubine by the leader of the Greek expedition against
Troy, Agamemnon, who was the brother of Menelaus

THE MAN WHO DREAMED OF FAERYLAND (1891)

Wherever he walks, nature signals to man, before his death, the existence of an ideal place of perfect love

This poem begins each stanza with a place near Sligo; there is,
obviously, a strong autobiographical element in it.

Dromahair also spelt Drumahair, a village in County Leitrim near Lough Gill
(Irish: *Dromdha Eithiar*, the ridge of the two demons); it was considered a
'gentle' place where supernatural manifestations could be expected to occur
world-forgotten isle probably a fairy paradise, akin to the first island to
which the immortal Niamh brought Oisin in Yeats's *The Wanderings of Oisin*
(1889)
Lissadell a barony in County Sligo (Irish: the fort or courtyard of the blind
man). The Gore-Booth family have had their home there since the
eighteenth century, the present house having been built in 1832. See 'In
Memory of Eva Gore-Booth and Con Markiewicz'
the hill of Lugnagall (see fourth stanza), Irish: Hollow of the Strangers
(Yeats thought it meant the Steep Place of the Strangers). Lugnagall is a
townland in the Glencar Valley in County Sligo
golden or the silver solar and lunar principles when fused symbolise
perfection; solar is represented by gold, lunar by silver. Notice the 'silver
heads' and 'gold morning' of the first stanza, the 'stormy silver' and 'the
gold of day' of the third. Yeats is beginning to develop his repeated
symbols here, and this repetition enriches the picture of blessedness, of
perfection
Scanavin a townland a mile from Colloney in County Sligo; a well there is
called in Irish the well of fine shingle
spired the word implies spiral movement

This collection of poems published in 1899 had extensive notes by Yeats on his source material in Irish legends. The poems are **Symbolist**, melancholic, and full of haunting beauty, of longing and complaint and of frustrated love. The personages of early versions, Aedh, O'Sullivan Rua, Mongan, Hanrahan and Michael Robartes, were later replaced by 'He'.

THE HOST OF THE AIR* (1893)

O'Driscoll dreams that Bridget his bride has been taken away by another and awakens to the sound of mournful piping

Originally called 'The Stolen Bride'. Yeats's note gives the source of the poem as 'a Gaelic poem on the subject' which an old woman at Balisodare, County Sligo repeated to him and translated. He always regretted not having taken down the words. He explained in a note that anyone who tastes 'faery' food or drink is 'glamoured and stolen by the faeries' and that is why Bridget sets O'Driscoll to play cards. She had been swept away by the faeries, the 'folk of the air', in an early version of the poem.

Hart Lake a small lake in the Ox Mountains in County Sligo

Bridget his bride in another note (*Later Poems*, 1924) Yeats commented that in the Irish **ballad** the husband came home to find the Keeners, those mourners who utter the keen (from the Irish: *caoinim*, I wail) for the dead at wakes or funerals, lamenting, and thus knew his wife was dead

red wine ... white bread ... host of the air the 'host' in the Eucharist is the bread, the body of Christ. Here Yeats is blending pagan and Christian symbolism

THE SONG OF WANDERING AENGUS (1897)

A fish is transformed into a beautiful woman whom Aengus spends the rest of his life trying to find

This poem deals with the shape-changing of the fairies, the Tuatha de Danaan. It was, however, suggested to Yeats by a Greek folk song, probably 'The Three Fishes' in Lucy Garnett, *Greek Folk Poesy*

(1896), but when he wrote it, he was, he said, thinking 'of Ireland and of the spirits that are in Ireland'.

l Yeats's note on 'He mourns for the change that has come upon him and His Beloved, and longs for the End of the World' explained that the 'man with a hazel wand' in that poem 'may well have been Aengus, Master of Love'. Elsewhere Yeats called him the god of youth, beauty and poetry who ruled in Tir-na-nOg, the country of the young. He regarded him as full of enthusiasm, like both Hermes and Dionysus in Greek mythology

hazel wand the hazel was the Irish tree of life or knowledge and Yeats said that in Ireland 'it was doubtless, as elsewhere, the tree of the heavens'

glimmering girl ... apple blossom the image suggests Maud Gonne, with whom Yeats associated blossom and particularly apple-blossom. In his *Autobiographies* he described their first meeting when her complexion 'was luminous, like that of apple-blossom through which the light falls and I remember her standing that first day by a great heap of such blossoms in the window' (p. 123)

silver apples ... golden apples compare the imagery of these lines with their lunar and solar imagery with that in 'The Man who Dreamed of Faeryland'

THE SECRET ROSE   (1896)

A hymn to the Rosicrucian symbol of rose and cross, and to the rose itself, emblem of love

This poem blends pagan and Christian symbolism. It also reflects Yeats's membership of the Hermetic Order of the Golden Dawn and the symbols and rituals of the Order and of Rosicrucianism.

Rose ... great leaves the Rosicrucian emblem of the four-leaved rose is probably intended here and suggests the mystic marriage of rose and cross. Yeats had a vague belief in the possibility of some revelation occurring; it was bound up with his idea of creating an Order of Celtic Mysteries (in which he might establish complete understanding with Maud Gonne). The Rose also suggests the Red Rose or Intellectual Beauty, and Ireland and Maud Gonne. He gave the title *The Secret Rose* to a volume of his stories published in 1897

Holy Sepulchre the tomb of Jesus Christ in Jerusalem

the ... Magi the three wise men who came from the east to attend the birth of Jesus, bringing with them gifts of gold and frankincense and myrrh

the king whose eyes / Saw ... / In Druid vapour Yeats's note tells us that he unintentionally changed the story of the death of Conchubar, king of Ulster, who did not see the crucifix in a vision but was told of it. He had been wounded by a ball made of the dried brain of an enemy which lodged in his head and was left there; his head was mended with thread of gold, and he survived for seven years. Then, noticing 'the unusual changes of the creation and the eclipse of the sun and the moon at its full' and asking Bucrach the Druid the reason for this, he was told that Jesus was being crucified, whereon he drew his sword, saying he would kill those who were putting Jesus to death, and began to cut and fell a grove of trees. The excessiveness of his fury caused the ball to burst out of his head and he died

pierced hands ... rood those of Christ, nailed to the rood, the Cross

him / Who ... Fand ... Emer in Irish legend, two birds linked with a chain of gold sang the army of Ulster into a magic sleep: the birds turned into two beautiful women and cast a magical weakness on the hero Cuchulain in which he lay for a year. Then Aengus ('probably Aengus, the master of love') came and told him that Fand, wife of Mannannan MacLir, master of the sea, loved him, and that she and her sister Laban would heal his magical weakness if he would come to the country of the gods. He did so, and, after being Fand's lover for a month, promised to meet her at a place called 'the Yew at the Strand's End'. He returned to earth, but his wife Emer won his love back, and Mannannan carried Fand off from 'the Yew at Strand's End'. Cuchulain went mad with grief when he saw her going, and wandered in the mountains without food or drink till a druid's drink of forgetfulness cured him. Yeats regarded the love story of Cuchulain and Fand as 'one of the most beautiful of the old tales'

him who drove the gods ... liss after the battle of Gabhra (near Garristown in north County Dublin) Caoilte, friend of Oisin, one of the Fianna or Fenians, when all the Fianna were killed, drove the gods out of their liss (a mound or fort) either at Osraighe (Ossory) or at Eas Ruaidh (Assaroe)

barrows burial places

proud dreaming king Fergus MacRoigh: see notes on 'Fergus and the Druid' above

him who sold tillage a young man in 'The Red Pony', a folk tale in William Larminie, *West Irish Folk Tales and Romances* (1893). He finds on the road a box with a light coming from it and a lock of hair inside it. He becomes the servant of a king, and leaves the box in a hole in the wall of the stable where the light from it is strong; he is asked to show the king the box, and is told to find the woman to whom the hair belongs. Finally the young man, not the king, marries her

shining loveliness the poem was written to Maud Gonne

great wind probably a reference to the end of the world

THE FIDDLER OF DOONEY* (1892)

The fiddler claims that he will pass more readily into heaven because he has made others happy

This probably was suggested by a blind fiddler, James Howley, who played the music for outdoor country dances, held at Dooney Rock (Irish: Dun Aodh, Hugh's Fort) on the shore of Lough Gill, County Sligo.

Kilvarnet a townland near Ballinacarrow, County Sligo

Mocharabuiee Mrs Yeats added a footnote to the 1950 *Collected Poems*: 'pronounced as if spelt "Mockrabwee"'. The Irish name means the Yellow Plain, the townland of Magheraboy, south-west of Sligo

Peter St Peter keeps the keys of the Gate of Heaven

from IN THE SEVEN WOODS (1904)

This was the first book published by Yeats's sister Elizabeth Corbet Yeats at her Dun Emer press. It included the long poems 'The Old Age of Queen Maeve' and 'Baile and Aillinn' which show Yeats moving to a new, more direct style. There is, however, a tired air about some of the poems in this volume, published in the year that Maud Gonne married John MacBride, in 1903, noticeable, for example in 'Never Give All the Heart', 'O Do not Love Too Long' and 'Under the Moon'. The poem which conveys this most clearly is 'Adam's Curse'.

R ED HANARAHAN'S SONG ABOUT IRELAND   (1894)

Hanrahan sings of Ireland and her sorrows, personified in the figure of Cathleen, daughter of Houlihan, in a wild windswept landscape

This does not share in the general mood of the poems of *In the Seven Woods* (which were written later). It was included in a story entitled 'Kathleen-ny-Houlihan' and it may owe something to James Clarence Mangan's poem 'Kathleen-ny-Houlihan', which personified Ireland as Kathleen. It is written to Maud Gonne, whose favourite poem it was. She later acted the title-role of Cathleen, the old woman who symbolises a freed Ireland, in Yeats's play *Cathleen-ni-Houlihan* (1902). The poem was strengthened in various revisions. In Yeats's *Stories of Red Hanrahan* (1905) it is clear that Hanrahan is thinking of Ireland and her sorrows and it is made obvious that the poem reflects the tragic patriotism of Catholic Ireland.

Red Hanrahan Hanrahan was a character invented by Yeats, a wandering Irish poet and schoolmaster, probably founded on Eoghan Ruadh O'Sullivan (1748–84) who had a varied career as a poet, schoolmaster, a wandering labourer, a tutor, a sailor in the navy, a soldier, and finally a schoolmaster again. His poems circulated in manuscript and oral tradition and were not published till 1901 (See notes to 'The Tower' on pp. 47–8)

Cummen Strand the southern shore of the Garavogue estuary, north-west of Sligo

left hand unlucky in Irish and in many other traditions

Knocknarea ... the stones ... Maeve Maeve, Queen of Connaught, was reputably buried under a cairn on Knocknarea, a mountain in County Sligo

Clooth-na-Bare Lough Ia (Irish: the Lough of the Two Geese) on Sliabh Daene (Irish: Bird Mountain), in County Sligo. Yeats described Cathleen as seeking all over the world a lake deep enough to drown her faery (Yeats usually spelt fairy as faery) life of which she had become weary until she reached the deepest water in the world in Lough Ia. He added in a footnote that Clooth-na-Bare should be Cailleac Beare, meaning the Old Woman Beare (or Bere, or Verah or Dera or Dhera). She was associated with many

places in Ireland, notably the megalithic monument of Sliabh Daene, not far from Lough Ia
Holy Rood the cross

Aᴅᴀᴍ's ᴄᴜʀsᴇ (1902)

The poet and his companions compare the effort of writing poetry with the effort of being beautiful and of loving, and find that they have grown weary of the latter

This poem was written to Maud Gonne and the occasion of its writing is discussed in her autobiography *A Servant of the Queen* (see notes below). It marks the emergence of more direct utterance, a nearer approximation to speech, in Yeats's work; while still carrying echoes of his romantic love poetry of the 1890s, it has a new note of tiredness, almost of disillusion about its insistence upon the need for hard work to create beautiful art and love.

Adam's Curse after Adam and Eve were expelled from the Garden of Eden (see Genesis 3:17–19) they had to live by their labour
We ... mild woman ... and you and I Yeats had called on Maud Gonne ('you'), who was staying at the house of her cousins May and Chotie Gonne in South Kensington, London, where her sister Mrs Kathleen Pilcher (that 'mild woman') was also staying. It was after dinner, the sisters were sitting beside each other on a couch, and Yeats (who considered Maud Gonne overworked and thought that she neglected herself) cast a critical eye on Maud, still in her dark clothes with the black veil she wore instead of a hat when travelling. As she put it, 'he told Kathleen he liked her dress and that she was looking younger than ever. It was on that occasion Kathleen remarked that it was hard work being beautiful which Willie turned into his poem "Adam's Curse"'
a moment's thought this quality of nonchalance, of an apparent casualness in the achievement of art, corresponds to *sprezzatura* (a careless rapture, a spontaneous improvisation), the quality Yeats admired in Renaissance figures in Italy. Elsewhere he stressed the difficulty of putting his thoughts and discoveries into rhyme (echoing a remark of William Morris about the hard work involved in writing poetry)

stitching and unstitching Yeats constantly wrote and rewrote his poetry, plays and prose, and when they were in print he continued to revise much of them in subsequent editions

labour to be beautiful elsewhere Yeats regarded the achievement of beauty ('the discipline of the looking glass') as one of the most difficult of the arts. God's punishment of Adam extended to Eve who was told that she would bring forth children in sorrow, suggested here by the word 'labour'

compounded of high courtesy love was a discipline, and had to be created and earned with reference to past achievements, to be approached wisely in 'the old high way of love'

from THE GREEN HELMET AND OTHER POEMS　　(1910 & 1912)

These are varied and transitional; they reveal the poet's greater readiness to write about public matters; and they record how his romantic poetry (and the hopes it conveyed) inspired by and written to Maud Gonne had foundered on her marriage to John MacBride in 1903. There is a static quality about the work of this volume, but one that is regretful and poignant. The poetry is being stripped of decoration.

No SECOND TROY 1908　1910
(See Extended Commentaries – Text 2)

UPON A HOUSE SHAKEN BY THE LAND AGITATION　　(1910)

The poet argues that to lose a big house redolent with culture and intellect is a worse loss than a number of small ones

This poem deals with the effects of the settlement of the Irish land question in the late nineteenth century and early twentieth, by a series of acts which culminated in the Wyndham Land Act of 1903 and the Ashbourne Act of 1909. Through this legislation, which had been forced on the British government by agrarian unrest and the work of Michael Davitt's (1846–1906) Irish Land League as well as the political skills of Charles Stewart Parnell (1846–91), the tenants were able to buy their farms. Landlords were given cash for their land, the tenants repaying the purchase price to the Government over a long period of time. In this poem Yeats reflects upon the effect of a reduction of rents made by the courts upon the Gregorys' Coole Park and the Gregorys' life based upon the estate.

How should ... this house in a prose draft for the poem Yeats wrote 'How should the world gain if this house [Coole Park, the home of the Gregory family, a 'Big House' in Co Galway] failed, even though a hundred little houses were the better for it, for here power has gone forth, or lingered giving energy, precision; it gives to a far people beneficent rule; and still under its roof loving intellect is sweetened by old memories of its descents from far off; how should the world be better if the wren's nest flourish and the eagle's house is scattered?'

passion and precision after reading the metaphysical poetry of John Donne (1571/2–1631) Yeats thought 'the more precise the thought, the greater the beauty, the passion'

lidless eye ... loves the sun refers to a belief that only an eagle can stare into the sun without blinking

eagle thoughts the eagle symbolises an active, objective person

Mean roof-trees of the cottages whose inhabitants would benefit from having to pay lowered rents

govern men reference to Sir William Gregory (1817–92), the husband of Yeats's friend Lady Gregory (1852–1932), playwright, translator and co-founder of the Abbey Theatre

a written speech a compliment to Lady Gregory, particularly for her books of Irish legends and her translations of Irish tales, *Cuchulain of Muirthemne* (1902) and *Gods and Fighting Men* (1904). She wrote in Hiberno-English, an English based upon the language used by local people, the Kiltartan dialect which had echoes of their former use of Irish

from RESPONSIBILITIES (1914)

Some of these poems record Yeats's disillusionment with Irish politicians, patrons and people; he now writes in passionate public speech, satirically and bitterly recording how his hopes for a regenerated Ireland were disappointed. Disappointed, too, were his hopes for a happy life with Maud Gonne, but his love poems, while they record the past, the old memories of her, with compassion and acceptance, still reveal how moved he was by her beauty and her regard for the people, who had turned on her. He records his delight in the achievement of art when it was fostered by enlightened and imaginative Italian patrons in the Renaissance. He rejects those who echoed the **Celtic Twilight** poetry he had written before the turn of the century, and he writes some superb poems out of his own emotional experiences, such as 'The Cold Heaven'. The poems about hermits, beggars and rogues may have been influenced by Synge's plays.

INTRODUCTORY RHYMES: PARDON, OLD FATHERS ...   probably 1913

Yeats celebrates his 'old fathers', his ancestors

This was prompted by malicious remarks about Yeats and his family made by George Moore, the Irish novelist, in an article in the *English Review* in January and February 1914. Yeats took his revenge on Moore (after Moore's death) in *Dramatis Personae* (1935).

Old Dublin merchant ... ten and four probably Benjamin Yeats, grandson of Jervis Yeats (d.1712), a Dublin linen merchant of Yorkshire stock, the first Yeats to settle in Ireland. Benjamin Yeats (1750–95), Yeats's great-great-grandfather, was also a Dublin linen merchant like his father and grandfather: he had the privilege of being allowed a discount on the excise of ten per cent on wine and tobacco and six per cent on other goods. Yeats's note of 1914 states that he could not correct his 'free of the ten and four' without 'more rewriting than I have a mind for'

Galway into Spain there was a good deal of trade between Galway in the west of Ireland and Spain in the eighteenth and nineteenth centuries

Old country scholar Rev. John Yeats (1774–1846), Rector of Drumcliff, County Sligo, the poet's great-grandfather. He was a friend of Robert Emmet (1778–1803) who led a rebellion in 1803 and was publicly executed in Dublin

Merchant and scholar Benjamin Yeats and the Rev. John Yeats

huckster's as opposed to those of the merchant and scholar

A Butler or an Armstrong Benjamin Yeats married Mary Butler in 1773, and the family prided themselves on this link with the distinguished Irish Butler family; the Dukes of Ormonde descended from Prince John's butler. The Rev. William Butler Yeats (1806–62), the poet's grandfather, married June Grace Corbet, whose mother's family, the Armstrongs, had military traditions

Boyne / James ... the Dutchman James II was defeated at the Battle of the Boyne (1690) by William of Orange. Yeats thought, erroneously, that some of his ancestors had fought for James; the error in earlier versions of the poem was corrected in 1929

Old merchant skipper William Middleton (1770–1832) of Sligo, the poet's maternal great-grandfather, who had a depot in the Channel Isles, and traded between Sligo and the Iberian peninsula

silent and fierce old man William Pollexfen (1811–92), the poet's maternal grandfather, a retired sea captain and head of the firm of Middleton & Pollexfen, Sligo

a barren passion's sake Yeats's unrequited love for Maud Gonne

close on forty-nine the poem was published in May 1914; Yeats was born on 13 June 1865

TO A WEALTHY MAN WHO PROMISED A SECOND SUBSCRIPTION TO THE DUBLIN MUNICIPAL GALLERY IF IT WERE PROVED THE PEOPLE WANTED PICTURES* (1913)

This polemic poem contrasts the behaviour of contemporary Irish patrons with those of the Italian Renaissance

Sir Hugh Lane, nephew of Yeats's friend Lady Gregory, had offered his valuable collection of French impressionist paintings to Dublin on condition they should be properly housed. He favoured a bridge site over the River Liffey designed by the famous English architect Sir Edwin Lutyens. In disgust at the reaction of Dublin Corporation to his proposed gift he placed the pictures in the National Gallery, London, and left them in his will to London. However, he had added a pencilled codicil, leaving the pictures to Dublin, before embarking on the *Lusitania* bound for New York;

the ship was torpedoed by a German submarine and he went down with it. The codicil was not properly witnessed and the pictures were retained in the Tate Gallery, London, until 1959 when a compromise agreement was reached by the British and Irish Governments; the pictures are now shared between London and Dublin.

You Lord Ardilaun, who thought private patrons should contribute to the cost of the proposed gallery if there was a public demand

Paudeen's ... Biddy's (diminutives) Padraig (Patrick), Bridget; both are used contemptuously here

some ... evidence see note on 'You' above

blind and ignorant town Dublin – and those of its newspapers which had attacked Lane's offer

Duke Ercole Duke Ercole d'Este (1431–1505), Duke of Ferrara, known for the brilliance of his court in art and letters. Yeats read of him in translations of Castiglione's *The Book of the Courtier* (1528). In 1907 Yeats first visited Italy and saw Ferrara and Urbino

his Plautus the Duke, who was a patron of the theatre, had five plays of the Latin comic dramatist Plautus (*c*.250–184BC) performed at his son's wedding in 1502

Guidobaldo Guidobaldo di Montefeltro (1472–1508), Duke of Urbino

That grammar school of courtesies ... Urbino's ... hill the refinement of his court at Urbino, situated on the slopes of the Apennines, and the good manners of his courtiers were praised by Castiglione in *The Book of the Courtier*

they drove out Cosimo Cosimo de Medici (1389–1464), the banker, statesman, and patron of the arts who established the power of the Medici family in Florence. He was exiled to Venice in 1433, but returned to Florence within a year

Michelozzo's ... plan ... San Marco library Michelozzo de Bartolommeo (1396–1472), an architect who went to Venice with Cosimo de Medici, for whom he designed the Library of St Mark's, Venice and other buildings

SEPTEMBER 1913   (1913)

Romantic, rebellious Ireland has been replaced by a land of materialism and formalised religion

This was also provoked by correspondence in the Irish papers over the proposed Lane Gallery.

you the Irish people, particularly the newly prosperous middle-class Catholics

O'Leary John O'Leary (1830–1907) who had introduced Yeats to Irish writing in translation after he returned from Paris to Dublin in 1885; having spent five years of a twenty-year jail sentence for his part in the Fenian movement, he was released on condition he spent the next fifteen years out of Ireland. He was a dignified and well-read man who fitted Yeats's concepts of a romantic, idealistic nationalism

the wild geese those Irishmen who left Ireland (largely as a result of the Penal laws passed after 1691 which, among other prohibitions, debarred Catholic Irishmen from holding commissions in the British Army), to serve in the armies of Austria, France and Spain. About 120,000 'wild geese' are reputed to have left Ireland between 1690 and 1730

Edward Fitzgerald ... Robert Emmet ... Wolfe Tone Lord Edward Fitzgerald (1763–98) who served in America, became an Irish MP and was president of the military committee of the United Irishmen. He died of wounds he received while being arrested in Dublin. Robert Emmet who led an abortive rebellion in 1803 was tried for high treason and hanged publicly in Dublin. Theobald Wolfe Tone (1763–98) founded the United Irish Club, left Ireland, went to France from the United States, became a chef-de-brigade and led a French force to Ireland. He was captured at Lough Swilly and sentenced to death but committed suicide in prison. All three were protestants

TO A SHADE   (1913)

The poet, addressing a dead Irish patriot, berates the current shabby behaviour of one of his adversaries

This is another expression of discouragement, reflecting upon the reaction of the Irish public to Lane's offer of his pictures to

Dublin, and possibly influenced by Swift's poetry. It links the treatment of Lane with that accorded earlier to the Irish political leader Parnell, and to Synge over *The Playboy of the Western World*: these were the two earlier controversies that had stirred Yeats's imagination.

To a Shade Yeats is addressing the ghost of Charles Stewart Parnell, head of the Irish party at Westminster who was repudiated by Gladstone, the Irish hierarchy and the Irish party, after having been named as co-respondent in the divorce case brought by Captain O'Shea against his wife
monument at the north end of O'Connell Street, Dublin
gaunt houses of Dublin
they the Irish people and their leaders
A man Sir Hugh Lane. See 'To a Wealthy Man ... Pictures'
Your enemy William Martin Murphy (1844–1919), proprietor of two Dublin papers, *The Irish Independent* and the *Evening Herald*. He opposed the Lane benefaction; he had earlier opposed Parnell and supported Tim Healy who led the attack on him within the Irish party
set / The pack probably a reference to the influence wielded by Murphy's two papers. It may reflect a phrase of Goethe's, quoted during the controversy over Parnell's grave, comparing the Irish to a pack of hounds 'always dragging down some noble stag'
Glasnevin coverlet Glasnevin cemetery north of Dublin, where Parnell is buried

A COAT   (1912)

The poet compares his old style of writing to an embroidered coat, which others now wear as their own. He would rather go naked

This marks Yeats's full renunciation of his early Celtic Twilight style. He resented its continuation by other, lesser poets.

I made my song a coat I made a coat for my song
old mythologies the Irish legends and tales he had read in nineteenth-century translations such as those of O'Donovan, O'Curry, O'Looney, Mangan and Ferguson and in Standish O'Grady's fiction and histories

the fools possibly a reference to the poets who had gathered round George Russell in Dublin – notably 'Seumas O'Sullivan' – who wrote in Yeats's early Celtic Twilight manner

from THE WILD SWANS AT COOLE   (1919)

These poems were mostly written between 1915 and 1918, but they were not placed in strictly chronological order. The volume contains poems which deal with the tower in the west of Ireland that Yeats bought in 1917: these poems are linked with the esoteric system of thought he was to set out in *A Vision* in 1926. They are cryptic but convince through their strength and assurance. The poet is now prepared to write on such subjects as his friends and acquaintances (in the **elegy** 'In Memory of Major Robert Gregory', for instance), and on the effects of age; but he is moving away from the bare poetry of, say, *The Green Helmet* and *Responsibilities*.

THE WILD SWANS AT COOLE   (1917)

The life of the wild swans, seen for the first time nineteen years before, seems constant and immutable compared with the poet's own life

This records how Yeats's life has changed since he first stayed at Coole Park, County Galway, in 1897. When he first stayed there he was 'involved in a miserable love affair [with Maud Gonne], that had but for one brief interruption absorbed my thoughts for years past, and would for some years yet'; now he realises romantic love cannot be rekindled.

nine-and-fifty swans there *were* fifty-nine of them; Yeats made a careful count
nineteenth autumn the poem was written in 1916. Yeats regarded 1897 as a turning point in his life
The first time he had visited Coole briefly in 1896, but first stayed there in 1897, and was to spend his summers there till his marriage. Lady Gregory's orderly household provided him with ideal conditions for writing; he

benefited from the regular routine she imposed, the kindness he received
there

my heart is sore … lover by lover … grown old the swans mate for life, but,
in contrast, Yeats is thinking of the death of his love for Maud Gonne (and
possibly thinking that Iseult Gonne, her daughter, to whom he proposed
marriage in 1916 and 1917, might consider him an old man); his heart,
unlike those of the swans, has grown old

By what lake's edge the swans did not nest at Coole – the first time Yeats
knew them to do so was thirty years after his first stay at Coole

IN MEMORY OF MAJOR ROBERT GREGORY (1918)

The poet sets out to recall old friends who are now dead but the memory of a recent death makes it too painful to continue

This had this note after the title: 'Major Robert Gregory RFC,
MC, Legion of Honour, was killed in action on the Italian Front,
January 23, 1918.' (He was shot down in error by an Allied pilot,
but this was not known until later.) This poem records other
friends that were dead, and links Gregory with Thoor Ballylee,
the tower at Ballylee in County Galway (near Coole Park) that
Yeats bought for £35 in 1917 and lived in every summer up to
1929.

almost settled at the time Yeats wrote the poem he and his wife (he married
Georgie Hyde Lees in 1917) were living near the tower in Ballinamantane
House which Lady Gregory had lent them

our house Yeats called the tower Thoor (Irish: *tor/twr/tur*, tower) Ballylee

turf Irish: peat, used in English speech there

Lionel Johnson Johnson (1867–1902), whom Yeats met in 1888 or 1889,
was a minor poet, a member of the Rhymers' Club which met in The
Cheshire Cheese, a London Fleet Street chop-house

courteous to the worst Johnson was a drunkard, but impressed Yeats by his
poise and learning

much falling this may refer to Johnson's poem 'Mystic and Cavalier'
describing himself as 'one of those that fall' (but it may also refer to
Johnson often falling down in a drunken stupor! He died after a fall from a
bar stool)

John Synge John Millington Synge, an Irish writer, greatly impressed Yeats who wrote warm praise of his work. He first met Synge in Paris in 1896 and urged him to go to the (Irish-speaking) Aran Islands in the Atlantic Ocean, about thirty miles off County Galway, to write about the life of the islanders. Synge knew Irish and his plays *Riders to the Sea* and *The Playboy of the Western World* are based on his experience of the Aran Islands. His uncle had been a Protestant clergyman there

dying he suffered from Hodgkin's disease

stony place the Aran Islands

George Pollexfen Yeats's maternal uncle George Pollexfen (1839–1910), with whom he used to stay in Sligo when a young man, was a hypochondriac, who rode in steeple-chases in his youth, often in County Mayo

opposition, square and trine (astrology) heavenly bodies separated by 180o, 90o and 120o respectively. Pollexfen had become interested in symbolism, astrology and the supernatural

dear friend's dear son Lady Gregory's son Robert (1881–1918), subject of the elegy

Our Sidney Robert Gregory had a versatility similar to that of the Elizabethan poet Sir Philip Sidney who also died in action overseas. Gregory was educated at New College, Oxford and the Slade; he also worked in Paris at the atelier of Jacques Blanche, and exhibited in Chelsea in 1914. He was a good shot, a bowler, boxer and horseman; he joined the Connaught Rangers in 1915, and transferred to the Royal Flying Corps in 1916; he was awarded a Military Cross in 1917 for 'conspicuous gallantry and devotion to duty'

all things ... loved by him he had encouraged Yeats to buy the tower described in this stanza

he would ride a stanza added at the request of Gregory's widow

Castle Taylor ... Roxborough both in County Galway; Roxborough was the seat of the Persse family where Lady Gregory, born a Persse, grew up

Esserkelly ... Mooneen also places in County Galway, near Ardrahan

a great painter see Colin Smythe, *Robert Gregory 1881–1918* (1981), p. 10. This volume reproduces some of Gregory's work, which is not widely known

Clare rock Clare, a county south of County Galway, has much limestone

consume ... combustible the imagery may have been suggested by a phrase in a letter of Henry James to Yeats. Yeats thought (see his *Autobiographies*,

p. 318) the image of dried straw, burning quickly, represented violent energy which consumes nervous vitality. But the fire needed for the arts had to burn slowly

AN IRISH AIRMAN FORESEES HIS DEATH   (1919)

The poet enters the mind of Robert Gregory in the moments before his death in the air

See notes on 'In Memory of Major Robert Gregory' above. Another poem on his death, 'Reprisals', was not published until 1948.

I know Robert Gregory is the speaker
Those that I fight the Germans
Those that I guard the English or, possibly, the Italians
Kiltartan Cross a crossroads near Robert Gregory's home, Coole Park, County Galway
lonely impulse of delight Yeats thought that men like Gregory shared moods with great **lyric** poetry (with Wordsworth's 'Resolution and Independence'), their moods part of the 'traditional expression of the soul'

THE SCHOLARS   (1915)

The poet contrasts elderly scholars with young poets, instancing the shock a meeting with Catullus would induce in such scholars

This poem may reflect the influence of Ezra Pound, who acted as Yeats's secretary during part of 1913 and 1916.

Catullus the Roman love poet, Caius Valerius Catullus (?84–?54BC). After arriving in Rome in his early twenties Catullus had become infatuated with a woman about ten years his senior who had many lovers and played with his affections. His intense love and hate for her are shown in his poems to 'Lesbia'

THE FISHERMAN   (1916)

The poet draws a contrast between his ideal Irishman and the real men of his contemporary Ireland

him the imagined ideal man

Connemara clothes homespun tweed. Connemara is an area in County Galway, whose west coast borders on the Atlantic

And the reality the actual audience Yeats had met, described further in lines 13–24

The dead man probably Synge

great Art beaten down probably a reference to the reception of Synge's plays (Yeats was deeply disturbed by the riots at the performance of Synge's *The Playboy of the Western World* in 1907 and insisted on continuing to stage the play) and Lane's proposal for a gallery to house the paintings he intended to give to Dublin (see 'To a Wealthy Man ... Pictures')

a twelvemonth since Yeats wrote a prose draft for the poem between 18 and 25 May 1913 in the Maud Gonne Manuscript Book; the poem itself was dated 4 June 1914 in the same book

down-turn of his wrist Yeats was himself a skilled fly fisherman

THE PEOPLE   (1915)

The poet recalls a conversation between himself and Maud Gonne

The poem records a conversation between Yeats and Maud Gonne in which he told her how he might have lived in Italy writing, but had been caught up in work – 'all sorts of trouble and annoyance for a mob that knows neither literature nor art', as he put it in a letter of 1901 (see Yeats, *Letters* (1954), p. 356). She reproved him, saying that though the mob had turned against her (when it was known that she had instituted proceedings in France for a divorce from her husband) she never complained of the people.

all that work his work for the Irish literary movement, his political work for the 1798 Association, his work to create an Irish theatre and then, when the Abbey Theatre was established, his work as its manager

The daily spite ... of this unmannerly town Dublin, known for its savage gossip. 'Daily' may suggest the Irish newspapers' treatment of Parnell and Lane, and also possibly the hostile reception given to some of Yeats's and Synge's plays

most defamed possibly Yeats had in mind George Moore's malicious comments in *Hail and Farewell*

Ferrara wall ... Urbino Yeats had visited Ferrara and Urbino in 1907 on his first trip to Italy

the Duchess ... dawn here Yeats refers to Castiglione's *The Book of the Courtier*, which describes a prolonged evening's talk at Urbino that went on till dawn

my phoenix Maud Gonne. When first published (in *Poetry Chicago* in February 1916) the poem was entitled 'The Phoenix'. Another poem about her, 'His Phoenix', written in January 1915, was included in the same number of the magazine

set upon me probably a reference to Maud Gonne being hissed at in the Abbey Theatre in 1906 after her separation from her husband

After nine years as the poem was written in 1915, it is likely Yeats was thinking back to the incident mentioned above

BROKEN DREAMS* (1915)

The poet's former lover's beauty, now that she has aged, is a vague memory

Yeats hopes that after death he will see her as she was in youth. He imagines some older people recognising her, remembering her kindness, and younger ones wanting to know about the lady whom he celebrated in his poems.

EGO DOMINUS TUUS 1915 (1917)

A dialogue between the objective and the subjective, about the self and anti-self

The poem's title comes from Dante's *Vita Nuova*. In an essay, 'Per Amica Silentia Lunae', Yeats indicated that the poet or artist has an uncomprehended strength on which to draw. He described how Dante saw the 'Lord of Terrible Aspect' in his chamber but could only understand a few of the things told him, among them 'Ego dominus tuus' (Latin: I am your master) (*Mythologies*, pp. 325–6). The poem is cast as a dialogue between Hic and Ille (Latin: the one and the other, or this man and that man). Hic presents the objective, Ille the subjective, and the poem is concerned with Yeats's theory of the self and anti-self. Its meaning can be expanded by some of the contents of 'Per Amica Silentia Lunae'.

wind-beaten tower the poem is set at Yeats's tower in Ballylee, County Galway

A lamp a **symbol** of the search for wisdom. Compare the light in the tower in 'The Phases of the Moon' and the candle in 'Meditations in Time of Civil War II'

Michael Robartes a character invented by Yeats. He appears in various stories in *The Secret Rose* (1897), and is a mysterious person who has travelled in the Near East; he also appears in 'The Phases of the Moon' and is part of the myth-making in the Introduction to *A Vision* (1925)

Magical shapes in *A Vision* Robartes has traced many diagrams on the Arabian sands. He is reputed to have found in his travels an Arab tribe of Judwalis who remember the doctrine of a Christian philosopher at the court of Harun Al-Raschid, Kusta ben Luka (an actual person)

my own opposite Yeats had developed a theory of the mask: by adopting a mask, by imagining ourselves different from what we are and attempting to assume that second self we can impose discipline, an active dramatic virtue, upon ourselves, see both his *Autobiographies*, p. 503, and *Mythologies*, p. 334

And I would find Hic's reply is to suggest that he prefers himself to an image of his opposite or anti-self. The 'And' is, in effect, 'But', an objection to Ille's summoning his opposite

gentle, sensitive mind Yeats saw a contrast between his own time and that of the Middle Ages and the Renaissance, when, he thought, people modelled themselves on Christ or some classic hero. Thus the modern period seemed to him critical rather than creative, because it looked at itself in a mirror rather than meditating upon a mask (or its opposite) (See his *Mythologies*, p. 333)

Dante ... the most exalted lady Dante said he fell in love with Beatrice – 'the apple on the bough', probably Beatrice Portinari (1266–90) – when he was nearly nine, and she eight years and four months old. She married Simone dei Bardi. Yeats thought Dante celebrated 'the most pure lady poet ever sung' but recorded that he had, in Boccaccio's phrase, 'room among his virtues for lechery'

Lapo and ... Guido probably Lapo degli Uberti (the son of Manente degli Uberti, called Farinata, Chief of the Florentine Ghibellines; a wise and brave man who died in 1264, a year before Dante was born), or, less likely, Lapo

Gioanni (*c*.1270–1330) and Guido Calvalcanti (*c*.1230–1300), Italian
poets, friends of Dante

Bedouin's ... roof the tent of a desert-dwelling arab

cliff probably Petra (in Jordan), a city carved from rock

The sentimentalist ... reality Yeats thought that 'practical' men, who
believed in money, position, marriage, activity at work or in play, were
sentimentalists. No artist he had read of, or known, seemed to him a
sentimentalist

Keats ... Luxuriant song John Keats (1795–1821) seemed to Yeats to have
had a thirst for luxury which he could only satisfy by imaginary delights

The phases of the moon   1918

Aherne and Robartes discuss the Great Wheel of the Lunar Phases

This poem, closely related to 'Ego Dominus Tuus', deals with one of the
major ideas later developed in *A Vision* (1925), the phases of the moon
(see diagram below). Two invented characters, Aherne and Robartes
discuss this beside Yeats's tower at Ballylee, County Galway, associated
with past towers and the search for wisdom in earlier literature.

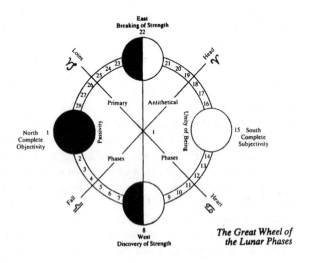

*The Great Wheel of
the Lunar Phases*

He and his friend Yeats was imagining that Robartes and Owen Aherne, another invented character from the stories of *The Secret Rose* (1897), had argued with him, an idea repeated in the Introduction to *A Vision* (1925)

Connemara cloth see notes on 'The Fisherman'

the far tower ... Platonist ... Shelley's visionary prince ... Palmer a reference to John Milton's (1608–74) *Il Penseroso* where the speaker wants his lamp to be seen at midnight 'in some high lonely tower' where he can study Hermes Trismegistus (a Greek name for the Egyptian god Thoth, credited with powers of magic and mysticism) and Plato (*c*.427–*c*.347BC), the Greek philosopher. Samuel Palmer (1805–81), the English visionary artist, illustrated Milton's *Shorter Poems* (1889) and depicted this tower illuminated by a waning crescent moon. It is likely that Percy Bysshe Shelley (1792–1822) echoed Milton's lines in his own 'Prince Athanase', a character who also studies wisdom 'in a lonely tower'. Yeats referred to this image in *Autobiographies*, p. 171, and in the essay 'Discoveries', *Essays and Introductions*, p. 294

Pater Walter Pater (1839–94), an English essayist and critic, known for his polished, involved prose style and his aesthetic sensibility. Yeats's own prose in the 1890s was elaborate and decorative

the phases of the moon see diagram, 'The Great Wheel of the Lunar Phases', from *A Vision*

The full ... crescents the full is the fifteenth phase, in *A Vision* one of complete subjectivity and beauty. The dark is the first phase, one of complete objectivity, a supernatural incarnation. The crescents are phases 2–14 and 16–28

six-and-twenty because phases 1 and 15 are not phases of human life

first ... half phases 2–8

towards the full phases 9–14

cat-o'-nine-tails a rope whip consisting of nine knotted thongs, used to flog prisoners

Athene ... Achilles an incident in Homer's *Iliad*, I, 197 or XXII, 330

Hector the eldest son of Priam, King of Troy, killed by Achilles in the Trojan War

Nietzsche Friedrich Nietzsche (1844–1900), a German philosopher interested in the idea of the superman. Yeats first read him in 1902, finding his ideas about the heroic stimulating; he may have supplied Yeats with an awareness of the value of gaiety

twice born, twice buried phases 13 and 14

the soul at war in *A Vision* phase 13 is where 'entire sensuality is possible' – the examples given are the French poet Charles Baudelaire (1821–67), the English artist Aubrey Beardsley (1872–98) and the English minor poet Ernest Dowson (1867–1900) – and the phase is one where **symbols**, **metaphors** and **images** morbidly preoccupy the people of the phase

the frenzy ... fourteenth moon *A Vision* gives Keats and the Italian painter Giorgione (*c.*1478–1511) as examples of the phase, and many beautiful women who include Helen of Troy. Intellectual curiosity is not strong in such persons, nor responsibility

thought becomes an image beings of this phase in *A Vision* have narrowed their circle of living, their efforts have ceased, their thoughts a series of separate images

Sinai's top Mount Sinai, where Moses received the Ten Commandments (see Exodus 19 and 20)

the man within Yeats, in the tower

the crumbling of the moon phase 16 when there is aimless excitement, incapable idealism within such beings, examples of whom are given in *A Vision* as William Blake, the English poet, artist and engraver (1757–1827), the French satirist François Rabelais (?1494–?1553), the Italian poet Pietro Aretino (1492–1557), the Swiss-German alchemist Paracelsus (1493–1541) and some beautiful women

from MICHAEL ROBARTES AND THE DANCER (1921)

Some of the poems in this volume show the effect of marriage on Yeats: 'Solomon and the Witch' reveals how close Mrs Yeats was to Yeats's thoughts, and reflects the confidence her automatic writing brought to his writing *A Vision*. 'Under Saturn' pays tribute to the wisdom that she brought to the marriage, the comfort she had made for her husband. Other poems, 'An Image from a Past Life' and 'Towards Break of Day' also deal with their relationship. *A Vision* provided powerful new metaphors and symbolism for Yeats's poetry, as 'Demon and Beast' and 'The Second Coming' demonstrate. The violence that followed the Easter Rising in 1916, itself so precisely and poignantly recorded in the personal reaction of 'Easter 1916', continued to disturb Yeats, as 'A Prayer for my Daughter' indicates in its prayer for custom and ceremony, out of which innocence and beauty are born.

MICHAEL ROBARTES AND THE DANCER* 1919

A dialogue between 'He' and 'She', in which 'He' urges his listener to pay great attention to her beauty

He and She represent Yeats's and Iseult Gonne's views. The poem urges young girls to make beauty their aim and consideration, citing the paintings of Veronese and Michelangelo to prove the ultimate significance of the sensuous of sight and touch.

this altar piece probably a painting ascribed to Paris Bordone (c.1500–71) in the National Gallery of Ireland
Athene (Greek mythology) a virgin goddess of wisdom and practical skills
Paul Veronese the cognomen of the Venetian painter Paolo Cagliari (1525–88)
the lagoon at Venice
Michael Angelo's Sistine roof Michelangelo Buonarrote's (1475–1564) painted ceiling in the Sistine Chapel in the Vatican
'Morning' and his 'Night' statues by Michelangelo in the Medici Chapel, San Lorenzo, Florence which Yeats saw on his visit there in 1907
wine and bread a reference to the Eucharist, the Christian communion service, based on Christ's last supper when he gave the disciples the Passover bread and wine (see Matthew 26, Mark 14, Luke 22)

UNDER SATURN 1919

The poet returns to his childhood haunts after twenty years away

This poem describes the first visit Yeats made with his wife to Sligo. The title implies a gloomy (saturnine) mood. Yeats excuses this mood: he praises his wife's wisdom and the comfort she has brought into his life, explaining that he is not thinking of his past love for Maud Gonne but is contemplating his youthful desire never to leave Sligo when he remembers his long dead relatives there.

lost love Yeats's love for Maud Gonne

the wisdom that you brought possibly a reference to Mrs Yeats's share in the making of *A Vision*

an old cross Pollexfen Yeats's maternal grandfather, William Pollexfen, a sea captain, shipowner and merchant in Sligo. See notes on 'Introductory Rhymes'

a Middleton one of Yeats's Middleton relatives in Sligo; William Pollexfen had married Susan Middleton, daughter of a sea captain and smuggler. Probably her brother William Middleton (1820–82), Yeats's great-uncle, is intended here

red-haired Yeats Yeats's paternal grandfather, the Rev. William Butler Yeats, a rector in County Down

Easter 1916   1916

The poet's reactions to the Easter Rising which he feels has changed everything

This poem was written when Yeats was staying with Maud Gonne MacBride at Les Mouettes, Calvados. In it he records his reactions to the Easter Rising in Dublin, when the centre of Dublin was occupied on 24 April by a force of about 700 members of the Irish Republican Brotherhood, led by Patrick Pearse, and members of the Citizen Army, led by James Connolly. They held out until 29 April; fifteen of their leaders were sentenced by courts martial and executed between 3 and 12 May. Yeats felt that the work of years – the bringing together of different classes, the freeing of Irish literature from politics – had been overturned by the violence, and he was extremely despondent about the future.

I have met them Irish revolutionaries, before the Easter Rising

grey ... houses many houses in Dublin were built of granite or limestone

the club probably the Arts Club in Dublin, of which Yeats was a founder member in 1907

Motley the particoloured garments of a jester or professional fool

That woman's days she was Constance Gore-Booth (1868–1927) of Lissadell, County Sligo, who married Count Casimir Markievicz. She took part in the Rising, but her sentence of death was commuted to penal servitude for life; she was released in an amnesty in 1917

young and beautiful Yeats first met her and her sister in 1894. See 'In Memory of Eva Gore-Booth and Con Markiewicz' and 'On a Political Prisoner'

This man Patrick Pearse (1879–1916). A member of the Irish bar, he founded St Enda's School for Boys, wrote propaganda poetry, edited *An Claidheamh Soluis* (The Sword of Light), and was Commandant General and president of the provisional government in Easter week; he surrendered in the Post Office

This other Thomas MacDonagh (1878–1916) a poet, dramatist, critic and university lecturer, author of *Literature in Ireland* (1916)

This other man ... a drunken vainglorious lout John MacBride, Maud Gonne's husband, who had earlier fought in South Africa with the Boers against the British. In 'The Grey Rock', written before 1913, Yeats had put words in the mouth of 'a woman [Maud Gonne] none could please': "In two or three years / I needs must marry some poor lout"

most bitter wrong to Maud Gonne. The most unpleasant circumstances which led Maud Gonne to seek a divorce from him are told in Nancy Cardozo, *Maud Gonne: Lucky Eyes and a High Heart* (1979)

stone a **symbol** for those who devoted themselves to a cause, particularly a political cause, and became bitter and inhuman as a result

a stone of the heart probably a reference to the effect of revolutionary politics on Maud Gonne

needless death ... keep faith at first the Rising was not popular in Ireland. The Bill for Home Rule had received the Royal assent in 1914 but was suspended, the English government promising to put it into force after the war was over. In the 1914–18 war approximately 100,000 Irishmen were serving in the British forces

Connolly James Connolly (1870–1916), a trade union organiser and author, who organised the Citizen Army, was Commandant in the Post Office in the Rising, and Military Commander of the Republican forces in Dublin. He too was executed

green the Irish national colour

a terrible beauty the phrase implies that the martyrdom of the leaders shot by the British had altered everything and made a new Ireland inevitable

TOWARDS BREAK OF DAY*   1919

The poet records two dreams by himself and his wife

This poem records two dreams, dreamed by Yeats and his wife on the same night when they were staying at the Powerscourt Arms Hotel, in Enniskerry, County Wicklow. In his he remembers a waterfall on the side of Ben Bulben, the mountain overlooking Sligo, while in her dream Mrs Yeats sees a white stag on the mountainside.

A waterfall probably the waterfall which falls into the lake at Glencar, County Sligo

The marvellous stag of Arthur according to Mrs Yeats this was the stag in Malory's *Le Morte d'Arthur*, III.v. It appeared at the marriage feast of Arthur (the mythical king of Britain) and Guinevere, pursued by a white brachet (bitch hound) and thirty couples of hounds

DEMON AND BEAST*   1918

A gull and a duck reflect the pattern of hatred and desire in the poet's own mind

A description of the sensation of momentary blessedness, set in St Stephen's Green, Dublin. (At the time Yeats and his wife were renting Maud Gonne's house there, no. 73.) He envisages himself in the National Gallery of Ireland, close to St Stephen's Green, and thinks of portraits there which seem to welcome and encourage him. He stops beside the little lake in St Stephen's Green where a gull seems to reflect the pattern of perning and gyring he had imposed upon the hatred and desire that had long plagued him, but from which he had escaped – but only temporarily, a point made in the final stanza. In it he contemplates the sweetness achieved in the lives of monastic communities in Egypt. This 'sweetness' emphasises the 'sweet company' he himself enjoys in the second stanza.

That crafty demon ... beast possibly, Peter Ure suggested in 'Yeats's "Demon and Beast"', *Irish Writing*, 31, 1935, the demon of hatred and the beast of desire

perned in the gyre to pern is to move with a circular spinning motion. Yeats used a gyre as an illustration of the movement of civilisations (see 'The Second Coming' and 'The Gyres'); it can be described as the increasing spiral that can be traced conically, starting from a point and eventually expanding to a circle

Luke Wadding's portrait portrait by Jose Ribera (1588–1652) of an Irish Franciscan who became President of the Irish College at Salamanca in Spain, and founded the College of St Isidore in Rome where he died in 1657

the Ormondes portraits in the National Gallery, Dublin, of titled members of the Butler family with which the Yeats family was connected. See 'Introductory Rhymes'

Strafford Sir Thomas Wentworth, 1st Earl of Strafford (1593–1641), Lord Deputy of Ireland from 1632 to 1638; the portrait is also in the National Gallery

the Gallery the National Gallery of Ireland, Dublin

the little lake in St Stephen's Green, Dublin

green-pated bird a duck

barren Thebaid an area around Thebes in upper Egypt

Mareotic sea a region in Egypt where monasticism flourished

Anthony St Anthony of Coma (?240–345)

twice a thousand more St Anthony, known for his enthusiasm, had a considerable effect on the spread of monasticism

Starved probably Yeats derived this from the account of fasting given in J.D. Hannay's books, *The Spirit and Origin of Christian Monasticism* (1903) and *The Wisdom of the Desert* (1904)

THE SECOND COMING   1919

An apocalyptic vision of the collapse of civilisation into anarchy

Now one of the most quoted of Yeats's poems (especially lines 3–8), it expresses his sense of horror at what might happen to our civilisation. Here he uses his symbol of the gyres to great effect: when a civilisation has reached its fullest achievement (represented by the circle) an annunciation occurs, the arrival of a new god, at the point in the middle of the circle, the beginning of the reversal of all that has been achieved (which is symbolised by the circle's expansion). To achieve horror he uses Christian **imagery**: the Second Coming is not, however, that which Christians might expect, but the antithesis of all that has succeeded, been built upon the birth of Christ in Bethlehem, his life and death. The succession of civilisations is discussed in *A Vision* (p. 83).

The falcon it is tracing out a gyre as it ascends in widening circles: it may represent Christian civilisation moving further away from Christ (the falconer)

blood-dimmed tide ... the ceremony of innocence is drowned possibly a reference to the Massacre of the Innocents by Herod is suggested here, and possibly the ceremony of baptism

the Second Coming see Christ's prediction of this in Matthew 24:1–31 and St John's descriptions of the beast of the Apocalypse in Revelations

Spiritus Mundi (Latin) the spirit of the world; Yeats glossed it as 'a general storehouse of images which have ceased to be a property of any personality or spirit'

A shape ... lion body ... man probably the brazen-winged beast Yeats imagined (and described in the Introduction to his play *Resurrection*) as associated with 'laughing, ecstatic destruction'. It may also have been suggested by the beast of the Apocalypse in Revelation 17:8,11

twenty centuries Yeats thought the Christian era, like the preceding age, was likely to be 2,000 years in extent

rocking cradle Christ's birth in Bethlehem ushered in the Christian period of history

A PRAYER FOR MY DAUGHTER   1919

The poet prays for virtues in moderation, merriment and innocence for his newborn daughter

Written for Anne Butler Yeats, the poet's first child, born in Dublin on 26 February 1919. It was completed at the poet's tower at Ballylee, County Galway where it is set. In it Yeats considers what future he would wish for his daughter: he would like her to have beauty, but not the dangerous beauty of a Helen of Troy or an Aphrodite, which led them both to unhappy unions; courtesy, for that leads to the glad kindness Yeats finds in his wife; merriment;

and a life lived in 'one dear perpetual place'. He hopes she will avoid
hatred, particularly intellectual hatred (he regrets Maud Gonne's
opinionated mind) and desires a radical innocence for her soul, and
a marriage based upon custom and ceremony.

Gregory's wood Coole Park, the Gregorys' estate, was near by

the bridge it crossed the stream which ran against one wall of the tower

Helen ... a fool Helen of Troy, who ran away from her husband Menelaus,
King of Sparta, with Paris. Yeats may be thinking of Maud Gonne (with
whom the Helen symbol is associated) and her unfortunate marriage to John
MacBride

that great Queen Aphrodite, the Greek goddess of love, who was born of the
foam (Greek *aphros* means foam) and thus was 'fatherless': she married
Hephaestus, the lame smith and god of fire. It was she to whom Paris gave
the apple when he was asked to choose between the three goddesses, Hera,
Athena and Aphrodite. She had promised him the love of the most beautiful
woman in the world (Helen)

the Horn of Plenty (late Latin, *cornucopia*) in Greek legend Amalthea, the
goat that suckled Zeus, chief of the Olympian gods. Zeus gave her a
cornucopia: her horns flowed with nectar and ambrosia; the cornucopia was
a magical possession, allowing its owner to get anything he wanted out of it

For beauty's very self probably a reference to Maud Gonne

a poor man Yeats himself

a glad kindness a reference to Mrs Yeats

Prosper but little both Maud Gonne and Constance Markievicz had recently
been in prison

An intellectual hatred this stanza refers to Maud Gonne ('the loveliest
woman born') and her obsession with politics

from THE TOWER   (1928)

These poems reflect the complexity and the success of Yeats's life in
the 1920s – marriage, children, a fine house in Merrion Square in
Dublin, the tower in the west of Ireland for the summers were the
domestic basis for his public successes, which included his
becoming a senator of the Irish Free State and winning the Nobel
Prize for literature. There was bitterness in evidence, too, raging at

the coming of age and apprehension at the increase of violence in the world and the likelihood of ruin and decay. The poems show us Yeats writing freely about history and politics, about philosophy, friendship and love. Behind them is the structure of *A Vision*, completed in 1925, published in 1926. Yeats now saw himself as part of the Anglo-Irish tradition, echoing the outspokenness of, in particular, four earlier Irish writers: Swift and Berkeley, Goldsmith and Burke.

SAILING TO BYZANTIUM   1926
(See Extended Commentaries – Text 4)

THE TOWER 1925

The poet rages against old age

This was written when Yeats was sixty. The first section suggests that now his body is ageing his attention should turn to philosophy. The second lists people connected with the tower or its neighbourhood and wonders whether they, too, resented the coming of age. The third section declares his faith in poets' memories rather than philosophers' thoughts.

SECTION I

Ben Bulben a mountain to the north of Sligo

Plato Yeats began to read him, probably in Thomas Taylor's translation of 1804, in the 1890s. Plato (*c*.427–348BC), pupil and admirer of Socrates, taught in the Academy at Athens where he composed his *Dialogues* in some of which Socrates figures. Plato accepted the possibility of a common good; he thought man could only make the best of himself in a well-ordered state. His doctrine of ideas implied that what we consider actual things are not real but 'copy' real ideas or forms and thus have an incalculable element not present in real being which is free from imperfection

Plotinus the Greek **Neoplatonic** philosopher (AD203–62). Yeats particularly admired Stephen MacKenna's translation of Plotinus, though he probably first read him in Thomas Taylor's *Five Books of Plotinus* (1794) and *Select Works of Plotinus* (1895)

SECTION II

the battlements of Yeats's tower

Mrs. French she lived at Peterswell nearby in the eighteenth century; Yeats read of the incident of the cutting of the farmer's ears in Sir Jonah Barrington's (1760–1834) *Recollections of His Own Time* (1918). See also his *Personal Sketches of His Own Times* (1827–33), pp. 26–7

Some few ... A peasant girl ... a song Mary Hynes, about whom Yeats wrote an essay, 'Dust hath closed Helen's Eye', in 1900; she had died at Ballylee sixty years before and he heard of her from several old people who lived in the neighbourhood. The song was written by Antony Raftery (1784–1834), the blind Irish poet, and was quoted by Yeats in his essay (see his *Mythologies*, pp. 24–5)

that rocky place Ballylee is in an area of limestone

fair a local market

drowned Yeats was told this by an old weaver

Cloone near Gort, County Galway

the man ... Homer the Irish poet Raftery and the Greek poet Homer were blind; each sang of a beautiful woman who was praised for her beauty by the old (the old men and women who remembered Mary Hynes had seemed to Yeats, remembering an incident in Homer's *Iliad*, to speak of her 'as the old men upon the wall of Troy spoke of Helen'). Helen acts as a link between the poets Raftery and Homer and Yeats himself who compared Maud Gonne to her

Hanrahan a character Yeats invented in the stories of *The Secret Rose* (1897) and *Stories of Red Hanrahan* (1904). He was a country poet, probably modelled upon the Irish poet Eoghan Ruadh O Suileabhan. This stanza and the next two retell the story 'Red Hanrahan' from Yeats's *The Secret Rose*

bawn possibly a misprint for barn: bawn means a fortified enclosure, a building

a man ... An ancient bankrupt this owner of the tower lived about a hundred years earlier, but the dates are uncertain

dog's day possibly an echo of Shakespeare, *Hamlet*, V.1.299, 'dog will have his day' or of the French poet Paul Fort, translated by Yeats's father's friend Professor York Powell: 'The dog must have his day', quoted by Yeats in *Essays and Introductions*, p. 498

certain men-at-arms ghosts, who had been seen playing dice in the room used as Yeats's bedroom in the tower
the Great Memory a stock of archetypal images
half-mounted man the bankrupt owner; the phrase implies he was not a gentleman, and probably comes from Sir Jonah Barrington
rambling celebrant Raftery, an itinerant Irish poet
The red man Red Hanrahan. The name was suggested to him, Yeats said, by a name he saw on a shop in a Galway village. There were many itinerant poets like Hanrahan in eighteenth-century Ireland
an ear the line is a pun, implying Mrs French was naturally musical as well as referring to Dennis Bodkin, the unfortunate farmer whose ears were cut off
The man drowned the farmer who fell into Cloone Bog on his way to see Mary Hynes
Old lecher Hanrahan
woman lost Maud Gonne

SECTION III

Burke Edmund Burke (1729–97), the Irish political philosopher, politician and orator. A member of the Westminster parliament, he advocated the causes of the Americans and the Irish Catholics; he impeached Warren Hastings for his conduct of affairs in India, attacked the excesses of the French Revolution, formulated conservative principles and advocated the abolition of the slave trade
Grattan Henry Grattan (1746–1820), an Irish orator and MP in the Dublin parliament. In 1782 he carried an address demanding legislative independence for Ireland (that is, freedom from the Westminster parliament's decisions); the successful parliament known as 'Grattan's Parliament' sat during a brief period of prosperity in Ireland, but Grattan was unable to persuade his fellow Irish MPs to treat their Catholic fellow countrymen more liberally and ultimately he was unable to prevent the Act of Union (which abolished the Irish parliament in Dublin and gave seats to Irish members at Westminster) being passed in 1800
the fabulous horn the cornucopia, the Horn of Plenty; see 'A Prayer for my Daughter'
his last song swan song; the 'Last reach' echoes a poem by Yeats's friend T. Sturge Moore (1870–1944), 'The Dying Swan', quoted in Yeats's notes to the poem in *Collected Poems*, p. 533

Plotinus ... Plato   see notes on Section I above
daws   jackdaws
metal   the nature, the material make-up of a person
sedentary trade   writing
testy   irascible

MEDITATIONS IN TIME OF CIVIL WAR   1922–3

The poet reflects on the violent past of mellowed old houses, his tower, and a Japanese sword, and on the current civil war

This poem is made up of seven sections which (apart from the first, written in England in 1921) were composed in Ireland during the Civil War. After the Anglo-Irish treaty was signed in London in December 1921 and accepted by the Irish parliament in January 1922 the Republicans led by Eamon de Valera (1882–1975) refused to accept it, and civil war broke out between them and the government of the new Irish Free State. In this poem Yeats contemplates the violence that went into the creation of great houses, wondering whether the greatness vanishes when the violence and bitterness that made them have been dissipated by a succession of owners who have grown up in the gentleness created in those who inherit such houses. He thinks of his own tower and its past and of his children; he thinks, in Section III, of the **symbolism** of Sato's Japanese sword and of the skills, transmitted from father to son, that made it. In Section IV he thinks of what his descendants may or may not achieve, assessing the legacy, the legend of the tower. He was worried at the time he wrote the poem about whether he should bring the children to live in Ireland where they would inherit bitterness or leave them in England where they, because of their Irish tradition and family, would be in 'an unnatural condition of mind'. Then in Section V he describes the arrival of members of the Republican and the Free State forces, envious of their youth, their activity, their apparently careless attitudes to death. The sixth section gives a brilliant portrayal of the uncertainties of civil war, with 'no clear fact to be discerned'. In the last section he contemplates images of hatred and destruction, wondering if he could have taken part 'In something that all others understand or share' but returns to his own concerns, the preoccupation with abstract ideas, with occultism, that has lasted since his youth.

Section I: Ancestral houses

overflows ... rains ... mounts the image is that of a fountain

Homer see Section II of 'The Tower'

The ... jet of the fountain

Juno a garden statue of the Roman queen of the gods, probably based on a memory of the gardens of Lady Ottoline Morrell's house at Garsington, near Oxford, where Yeats had stayed as a guest

escutcheoned doors doors with (ornamental or, possibly, heraldic) plates or shields surrounding keyholes or door handles, protecting the surface of the door

Section II: My house

tower this is a description of Yeats's tower, Thoor Ballylee, County Galway. It was built by the de Burgo family and was called Islandmore Castle later, in 1585

Il Penseroso's Platonist ... candle see 'The Phases of the Moon'

Section III: My table

Sato's gift Junzo Sato had admired Yeats's poetry in Japan, heard him lecture at Portland, Oregon in 1920 (where Sato was studying the canning industry) and gave the poet a present of an ancestral ceremonial sword

Chaucer ... five hundred years Geoffrey Chaucer lived from c.1345 to 1400. The sword was made in 1420, if we go back 500 years from 1920. But in a letter Yeats wrote to his friend Edmund Dulac on 22 March 1920 he said that it had been made '550 years ago'

Juno's peacock the peacock was sacred to Juno, consort of Jupiter, as a symbol of immortality. No source has yet been put forward for the idea that the peacock's scream heralded the end of a civilisation

Section IV: My descendants

my old fathers presumably Yeats's father John Butler Yeats, his grandfather, the Rev. William Butler Yeats, his great-grandfather the Rev. John Yeats, all of whom were graduates of Trinity College, Dublin

a woman and a man Yeats's children, Anne Butler Yeats (b. 1919) and Michael Butler Yeats (b. 1921)

Primum Mobile the prime mover, part of the Ptolemaic system; it was a wheel, the motion of which was supposed to cause the nine inner spheres to revolve around the earth in twenty-four hours

an old neighbour's friendship Lady Gregory's house and estate, Coole Park, County Galway, were within walking distance of Yeats's tower

SECTION V: THE ROAD AT MY DOOR

Irregular a member of the Irish Republican Army, which opposed the Anglo-Irish Treaty and thus brought about Civil War in 1922. The Republicans blew up the bridge beside the tower in the autumn of 1922

Falstaffian after the fat Sir John Falstaff, Shakespeare's comic character in *Henry IV, Part 1* and *The Merry Wives of Windsor*

Lieutenant and his men members of the Irish Free State army, loyal to the newly established Dublin government

balls of soot the moorhen's chickens

SECTION VI: THE STARE'S NEST BY MY WINDOW

Stare's Nest stare is the west of Ireland name for a starling. One had built in a hole beside Yeats's window

We are closed in Yeats wrote a note of explanation: 'I was in my Galway house during the first months of civil war, the railway bridges blown up and the roads blocked with stones and trees. For the first week there were no newspapers, no reliable news, we did not know who had won nor who had lost, and even after newspapers came, one never knew what was happening on the other side of the hill or of the line of trees. Ford cars passed the house from time to time with coffins standing upon end between the seats, and sometimes at night we heard an explosion, and once by day saw the smoke made by the burning of a great neighbouring house. Men must have lived so through many tumultuous centuries. One felt an overmastering desire not to grow unhappy or embittered, not to lose all sense of the beauty of nature.'

SECTION VII: I SEE PHANTOMS OF HATRED AND OF THE HEART'S FULLNESS AND OF THE COMING EMPTINESS

Jacques Molay (1244–1314) Grand Master of the Templars, a military-monastic order which protected pilgrims on their way to the Holy Land; he was arrested in 1307 and burned in 1314

Magical unicorns probably a reference to Gustave Moreau's (1826–98) painting *Ladies and Unicorns*, a copy of which hung on a wall of Yeats's Dublin house in 1936
Brazen hawks they are in contrast to the previous images of the heart's fullness

NINETEEN HUNDRED AND NINETEEN   1919

The poet reflects on the violence of war, present and past, and on the cyclic progress of history

This poem was prompted by incidents which occurred during the fighting between the Irish Republican Army and the British forces combined with the Irish police force in 1919. In Section I Yeats evokes the unexpected brutality of war, moving from the destruction of ancient Athens's sacred olive and its artefacts to his contemporary Ireland, and then reverting to Athens. Section II considers the cyclic progress of history while Section III links the **image** of the swan with the futility of dreaming that mankind's mischief could be remedied, something emphasised in the bitterness of the weasel imagery of Section IV, while Section V mocks at achievement and Section VI provides images of supernatural violence and witchcraft returning again. (Sections II and III are omitted below.)

SECTION I

An ancient image this was the sacred olive in the Erechtheum at Athens supposedly created by the goddess Athena: it was created by her in her rivalry with Erechtheus to become the deity of the city, he having created the spring of salt water there
Phidias the Athenian sculptor (*c.*490–417BC), famous for his chryselephantine statues (of gold and ivory), notably of Athena and Zeus; he designed the marble sculptures of the Parthenon
grasshoppers and bees Yeats got the idea from the Greek historian Thucydides (*c.*460–400BC) and possibly from the English critic Walter Pater's *Greek Studies: a series of essays* (1895)
when young Yeats is referring to the 1880s in particular as well as to the general pre-1914 war period

no cannon compare Isaiah 2:4: 'they shall beat their swords into plowshares
... nation shall not lift up sword against nation, neither shall they learn war
any more.' See also Micah 4:3 and Joel 3:10

dragon-ridden ... drunken soldiery ... go scot-free references to atrocities
committed in County Galway by members of the Auxiliaries and the Black
and Tans. These were forces specially recruited by the British Government
for action in Ireland. Mrs Ellen Quinn was killed by the Black and Tans; the
Loughnane brothers were murdered and their bodies mutilated

that stump ... ironies ... grasshoppers ... bees see note above

SECTION IV

seven years ago 1912, when the Home Rule Bill was introduced

SECTION V

mock at the great probably an echo of 'Scoffers', a poem by William Blake
which combines the idea of mockery with the destructive force of the wind

SECTION VI

Herodias' daughters witches. Yeats wrote in a note to 'The Hosting of the
Sidhe' that the Sidhe journeyed in the whirling winds that 'were called the
dance of the daughters of Herodias in the Middle Ages, Herodias doubtless
taking the place of some old goddess'. Herodias (?14BC-?40AD) was the
niece and wife of Herod Antipas (?d.40AD), tetrarch of Galilee and Peraea.
She persuaded her daughter Salome to ask for the head of John the
Baptist

Robert Artisson ... Lady Kyteler he was an evil spirit in the fourteenth
century in Kilkenny, the incubus of Dame Alice Kyteler who, it was alleged,
sometimes appeared as a hairy black dog, or a cat, or an Ethiopian. She
was married four times, and it was alleged she poisoned her first three
husbands and deprived the fourth of his senses 'by philtres and
incantations'. She was brought before an Inquisition held in 1324 by the
Bishop of Ossory

THE WHEEL   1921

We look forward to each season in turn, but may in fact be longing for death

Written in the Euston Hotel when Yeats was waiting to board the
Irish mail train for Holyhead en route to Ireland.

THE NEW FACES   1912

Addressed to Lady Gregory, the poem reiterates the strength of their friendship and links with Coole Park

This poem was not published immediately, possibly because its reference to Lady Gregory's growing old may not have seemed tactful. She was forty-four when Yeats first met her at a party in London in 1894; he seems to have thought he first met her in 1896 when he first visited Coole Park (with its famous catalpa tree); he stayed there as a summer guest from 1897 till his marriage.

TWO SONGS FROM A PLAY   1926

The death and rebirth of Dionysus are linked to the Virgin Mary and the coming of Christianity, which will destroy the old civilisation

The latter stanza of II was probably written in 1930–1. The two songs are sung by the chorus of Musicians in Yeats's play *The Resurrection* (1931) which treats of Christ's first appearance to the Apostles after his crucifixion. The play expresses Yeats's myth that Christianity terminated one 2,000-year cycle and began another.

SECTION I

a staring virgin this stanza draws a parallel between the myth of Dionysus, the Greek god of drink and revelry, and the death and resurrection of Christ. Dionysus was the child of a mortal, Persephone, and the immortal god Zeus. The staring (as if in a trance because the happenings are preordained) virgin is the Greek goddess Athene who snatched the heart of Dionysus from his body after he had been torn to pieces by the Titans; she brought it to Zeus who killed the Titans, swallowed the heart and begot Dionysus again upon the mortal, Semele. See note on 'Semele's lad', p. 57

the Muses ... Magnus Annus ... play they treat the event as a play because the ritual death and rebirth of the God seems a recurring event, part of the recurring cycles of history. The Great Year, then, indicates a cycle of time

Another Troy ... Another Argo's these lines echo the prophecy of the Roman epic poet Virgil (70–19BC) in his fourth *Eclogue*, that Virgo, daughter of

Jupiter and Themis, last to leave the Earth at the end of the Golden Age, will return with her star, Spica, bringing back the golden age. (This was later sometimes called the 'Messianic Eclogue' and held to be a foretelling of the coming of Mary [as Virgo] and Christ). The *Eclogue* prophesies a second Troy and a second Greek attack on it, a second Argo. The Argo was the ship in which the hero Jason sailed on his quest for the Golden Fleece (the second fleece to be sought by a second Jason is Yeats's 'flashier bauble yet'). Yeats referred to the *Eclogue* several times in his prose, and was aware that Shelley had also drawn upon it in a chorus in his Hellas: 'The world's great age begins anew'

The Roman Empire ... appalled because the Christian message originating in the fierce virgin (Mary) and her Star (Christ) would overthrow the Empire. Thus Yeats is linking Athena, Astraea (the constellation Virgo) and Mary, Spica, Dionysus and Christ

SECTION II

that room the room where the last supper was eaten. See Matthew 26; Mark 14; and Luke 22

Galilean turbulence because Christ began his mission in Galilee. The 'turbulence' was foretold by astronomers in Babylon; they reduced man's status through their scientific views; and the Christian Church, according to Yeats, was to make man 'featureless as clay or dust'. In the second edition of *A Vision* (1937), pp. 273ff, he wrote that 'night will fall upon man's wisdom now that man has been taught that he is nothing'. The effect of Christianity, he argues here, is to nullify the achievements of classical civilisation

LEDA AND THE SWAN   1923

The myth of Leda's union with Zeus, in the form of a swan

This **sonnet** deals with the union of god and mortal, with the myth of Zeus, father of the Greek gods, taking the form of a swan and impregnating the mortal Leda, the wife of Tyndareus, King of Sparta. She bore the twins Castor and Pollux, and Helen, who subsequently married Menelaus, King of Sparta and, by running away with Paris, son of Priam, King of Troy, caused the Trojan war

and hence the sack of the city by the Greeks after a ten-year siege.
The myth of Leda's union with Zeus seemed to Yeats when he
began the poem to illustrate his idea that the effect of the French
Revolution had left Europe exhausted, and that 'Nothing is now
possible but some movement, or birth from above, preceded by
some violent annunciation'. As he played with the **metaphor** of
Leda and the Swan, he remarked, all politics went out of it. Leda is
analogous to the Virgin Mary. Each impregnation was the initiation
of a new age.

wall ... roof and tower of Troy
Agamemnon dead King of Argos, he led the Greek forces at Troy; he was the
brother of Menelaus. His wife Clytemnestra was a daughter of Leda by her
husband Tyndareus; while Agamemnon was at Troy she had an affair with
Aegisthus, and they murdered Agamemnon on his return to Argos

A MONG SCHOOL CHILDREN   1926
(See Extended Commentaries – Text 5)

C OLONUS' PRAISE*   1927

A translation of a chorus in the Greek tragedy *Oedipus at Colonus* by Sophocles

Yeats's translation of *Oedipus Rex* by Sophocles was first staged
in December 1926 at the Abbey Theatre, Dublin, and his
translation of *Oedipus at Colonus*, also at the Abbey, in September
1927. Yeats, who did not read Greek, had first become interested
in translating Sophocles in 1911–12, using a crib, and Jebb's
translation, as well as his friend Oliver St John Gogarty's help. For
these later translations of the 1920s he used Paul Masqueray's
translations of the Greek into French, which Mrs Yeats read to
him.

Colonus an Attic deme or district, Colonus of the horses, a hill about a mile
north of Athens, and the birthplace of Sophocles. Its name came from the
fact that the god Poseidon who gave the gift of the horse to men was
worshipped there

Semele's lad Dionysus, son of the god Zeus and the mortal Semele. (See
'Two Songs from a Play'.) Semele was advised by Hera, the consort of Zeus,
who was in disguise, to test her lover's divinity by asking him to come to her
in his true shape. Semele did so, but was killed by the fire of Zeus's
thunderbolts; he put the unborn child Dionysus in his thigh, to be born at
full term. Dionysus went down to Hades, brought Semele back to earth and
she then became an Olympian goddess
gymnasts' garden a grove on the banks of the river Cephisus at Athens,
sacred to the hero Academus, and the site of the Academy which Plato
founded in about 386BC
olive-tree … Athene in Greek myth Athena, the patron goddess of Athens,
gave the olive as a gift to man during a struggle with Poseidon (see note on
'Colonus' above) for ownership of the land in Attica which she won; the first
olive grew on the Acropolis at Athens, the second at the Academy
the Great Mother Demeter or Ceres (a corn goddess) mourning for
Persephone, her daughter, carried into the underworld by Pluto (or Hades),
brother of Zeus and Poseidon. Persephone was given permission to spend
half the year with her mother on earth and half with Pluto: obviously
a vegetation myth which is concerned with the sowing and growing of
corn

OWEN AHERNE AND HIS DANCERS* 1917 (1924)

The narrator is tormented by his love for a young girl

This poem was written shortly after Yeats's marriage (on 20
October). Aherne, an invented character, appeared in Yeats's
stories and in 'The Phases of the Moon'. It records Yeats's
relationship with Iseult Gonne, Maud Gonne's daughter, who at
the age of fifteen proposed to Yeats. He asked her to marry him in
1916 and in 1917 when he was staying at her mother's house in
France. (He had proposed – yet again – to Maud in 1916 after her
husband was executed for his part in the 1916 rising; see notes on
'Easter 1916'.) In September 1917 he accompanied Maud and
Iseult to England, but told Iseult she must decide within a week
whether or not to marry him: if she decided not to (as she did) he
would marry a friend he had known for some years, Georgie Hyde
Lees.

the Norman upland Maud Gonne MacBride's house, Les Mouettes, was near Calvados, in Normandy

its love Iseult Gonne

that young child Iseult Gonne (1895–1954)

the woman at my side Mrs Yeats

fifty years he was fifty-two in 1917

A MAN YOUNG AND OLD* 1926, 1927

Love poems that reminisce on Yeats's relationships with Iseult Gonne (VI) and Maud Gonne (VIII)

(I and II refer to Yeats's love for Maud Gonne, III to his affair with Mrs Shakespear in 1896).

VI HIS MEMORIES

holy shows the phrase has a pejorative meaning in Ireland

Hector see note on 'The Phases of the Moon'

The first possibly Maud Gonne

She Helen of Troy

VIII SUMMER AND SPRING

halved a soul compare 'Among School Children', lines 13–17

from THE WINDING STAIR AND OTHER POEMS   (1933)

The poetry of *The Winding Stair* is perhaps more personal than that of *The Tower*. The winding stair derives from the stone stair in Yeats's tower but the winding stairs in towers are symbols which he compares to the 'philosophical gyres' (see notes on 'Demon and Beast'); he mentions in this connection gyres in 'Swedenborg, Thomas Aquinas and certain classical authors'. There are celebrations of friendships, condensations of memories, and dramatisation of the struggles between the self and the soul: the supernatural jostles with the earthy comments of Crazy Jane, and the eighteenth-century Irish writers receive noble praise. The tower is still present, and 'Byzantium' celebrates Yeats's image of the city in concentrated, rich imagery.

IN MEMORY OF EVA GORE-BOOTH AND CON MARKIEWICZ   1927

The poet recollects two girls, their beauty's decline and now their passing

Constance Markievicz had died in August of that year, her sister Eva the year before. Constance and Eva Gore-Booth grew up in Lissadell, a gaunt big stone neo-classical house in Sligo which Yeats visited in the winter of 1894–5. He had earlier known the girls as a child when living with his grandparents in Sligo. He enjoyed being a guest at Lissadell in 1894–5, as his letters record.

one a gazelle Eva (1870–1926) who wrote poetry, was interested in Neoplatonism and Indian mysticism, worked for the women's suffrage movement and became a social worker in Manchester

the older Constance (1868–1927), who studied art in Paris, married a Polish nobleman, also an artist, Count Casimir Markievicz. They settled in Dublin and she became deeply involved in revolutionary politics, joining the Citizen Army, training the Fianna Scouts, and taking part in the 1916 rising. Her sentence of death was commuted to life imprisonment; she was released in an amnesty in 1917, was the first woman elected to Westminster but did not take her seat. She became Minister for Labour in the first Dail Eireann, and was re-elected in 1921. She was several times imprisoned (see notes on 'On a Political Prisoner'). In the Civil War she supported de Valera, and won her seat back in 1923

lonely years she was estranged from her daughter: her husband and stepson had left Ireland; they did, however, return a few days before she died in 1927

gazebo possibly a summer house at Lissadell, or a place to look out from, but, most likely, in the Hiberno-English sense of the word – to make a gazebo of oneself, to look ridiculous – something of no value, a nonsense, something ridiculous. 'Gazebo' may have come into his mind from the sound echo of gazelle, a soft-eyed, delicately shaped antelope

DEATH 1927

The poet contrasts death of an animal with that of a man, and one man of superior worth, in particular

This was prompted by the assassination of Kevin O'Higgins (1892–1927), the Irish Free State's Minister of Justice (and a friend of Yeats) who was shot on his way to Mass. He had been in favour of the government's policy in the Civil War of executing anyone captured carrying arms and Yeats regarded him as the one man of strong intellect in the Free State government.

A DIALOGUE OF SELF AND SOUL 1927

'My Soul' warns that eternity beckons; 'My Self' still savours memories and physical remnants of the past

This may have been suggested by Andrew Marvell's (1621–78) poem 'A Dialogue between the Soul and the Body' which Yeats had read in *Metaphysical Lyrics and Poems*, ed. J.J.C. Grierson (1921).

winding ancient stair in Yeats's tower

consecrated blade the sword Junzo Sato gave Yeats. See 'Meditations in Time of Civil War'

embroidery the silk embroidery covering the sword

Montashigi Bishu Osafume Montashige who lived in the period of Oei (1394–1428) in Osafume, Japan

five hundred years ago see 'Meditations in Time of Civil War'

overflows ... basin compare the **imagery** in the opening stanza of 'Meditations in Time of Civil War'

blind ... ditches see the third stanza of Section II, and its 'blind man's ditch': the image comes from Matthew 15:14

A proud woman probably a reference to Maud Gonne

BLOOD AND THE MOON 1927

The poet has made the tower his own symbol, but are modern nations like it, half dead at the top?

This marks Yeats's interest in the Anglo-Irish literary and political tradition which he had been exploring in the 1920s. It is set in

Yeats's tower and finally questions whether modern nations are like the tower, half dead at the top. In Section II Yeats thinks of the Anglo-Irish writers he has come to appreciate. That Swift is among them suggests that Yeats in describing his own tower as half dead at the top may be thinking of Swift's remark, when gazing at a fine tree the uppermost branches of which were withered, 'I shall be like that tree, I shall die at [the] top'. The poem contemplates the effect of power – and death – and regards wisdom as the property of the dead.

this place Yeats's tower, Thoor Ballylee, County Galway

cottages rethatched by 1917 and adjoining the tower, they were used by Yeats and his wife as part of the tower's accommodation

Half dead at the top the restoration of the tower was not completed; the flat roof concrete, the top room 'a waste room' in Yeats's words

Alexandria's the Pharos at Alexandria, a lighthouse built $c.280$BC, one of the seven wonders of the world: it was destroyed by an earthquake in the fourteenth century

Babylon's Babylon, famous for its astronomers, was reputedly the site of the Tower of Babel. See Genesis 11:1–10

Shelley ... towers in his essay 'The Philosophy of Shelley's Poetry' Yeats described Shelley's use of towers (see also 'Ego Dominus Tuus' and 'The Phases of the Moon'). The reference is to 'the skiey towers' of *Prometheus Unbound* IV, 102–4: 'Where thought's crowned powers / Sit watching our dance ...'

this tower Yeats's tower

ancestral because Yeats is now discovering his intellectual ancestry in the Anglo-Irish writers whom he goes on to list: Oliver Goldsmith (1728–74); famous as the author of *The Vicar of Wakefield*, *She Stoops to Conquer*, *The Traveller* and *The Deserted Village*; 'the Dean', Jonathan Swift (1667–1745), the author of *The Battle of the Books*, *A Tale of a Tub* and *Gulliver's Travels* and many poems and satirical writings, who became Dean of St Patrick's Cathedral, Dublin; George Berkeley (1685–1753), philosopher and Bishop of Cloyne, County Cork; and Edmund Burke, political philosopher and politician. These Protestant Irish writers he regards as models to be placed against the general decline and degeneracy of contemporary Irish and English life

sibylline frenzy the frenzy of women oracles or prophetesses in antiquity, such as the Sibyl of Cumae, hence oracular or prophetic

the heart ... breast a reference to Swift's epitaph, written by himself in Latin, which Yeats translated as 'Savage indignation there / Cannot lacerate his breast', the Latin being *Ubi saeva Indignatio / Ulterius / Cor lacerare nequit*

the honey-pot probably an allusion to the periodical essays written by Goldsmith in *The Bee*

the State a tree a reference to Burke's *Reflections* (*Works*, II, 357) where he compares the state to an oak-tree that has grown through the centuries, an idea to which Yeats referred on several occasions

proved all things a dream Berkeley was an immaterialist philosopher

pragmatical, preposterous pig of a world ... its farrow it has been suggested that this phrase may stem from Yeats's experience as Chairman of the Commission on Ireland's coinage, when the artist who had drawn the sow and piglets for the halfpenny was asked to alter the sow's shape to a more marketable one

Saeva indignatio Swift's phrase; see note on 'the heart'

Seven centuries a reference to the age of the tower; see 'The Tower'

THE SEVEN SAGES 1931

This poem continues to meditate upon the four Anglo-Irish writers treated in Blood and the Moon'

The poem suggests that Yeats's ancestors must have known these writers (see his *Essays*, p. 298.) For Burke, Goldsmith, Berkeley, Bishop of Cloyne, Swift, see 'Blood and the Moon'. The 'Seven Sages' of the title, also known as the 'Wise Men of Greece' were: Solon of Athens (*c*.638–559BC), whose motto was 'Know thyself'; Chilo of Sparta (d. 597BC), whose motto was 'Consider the end'; Thales of Miletus (d. 548BC), whose motto was 'Who hateth suretyship is sure'; Bias of Priene (*fl.* 6th century BC), whose known saying was 'Most men are bad'; Cleobulus of Lindos (d. 564BC) who is known for 'The Golden Mean, or, Avoid extremes'; Pittacus of Mitylene (d. 570BC), whose advice was to 'Seize Time by the forelock'; and Periander of Corinth (d. 585BC) who said 'Nothing is impossible to industry'.

Grattan's house Henry Grattan, Irish parliamentarian; see Section III of 'The Tower'

tar-water Berkeley was a great believer in its efficacy as a remedy

Stella Swift's name for Esther Johnson (d. 1728), his friend from his days at Sir William Temple's house, Moor Park, in Surrey; she moved to Ireland with her friend Rebecca Dingley after Sir William's death. Swift's friendship with her lasted till her death; he wrote her many letters from London (the *Journal to Stella*) and poems on her birthdays

Whiggery the English Whig party; representative of the great aristocratic families and the well-to-do middle class, in the nineteenth century they represented a desire for reform on the part of the manufacturers and dissenters. Yeats regarded them as materialistic. He thought his four Anglo-Irish writers hated abstraction. (See his *Essays*, pp. 350–3 and 435–6)

Whether they knew it or not Burke and Swift were originally Whigs

Burke's great melody a reference to his speeches on the topics of the American colonies, Ireland, the French Revolution and the impeachment of Warren Hastings for his actions in India

COOLE PARK, 1929   1928

A tribute to Lady Gregory's role in Ireland's cultural history, and the function of Coole Park as a place where so many outstanding people met each other

A prose draft read: 'Describe house in first stanza. Here Synge came, Hugh Lane, Shaw Taylor, many names. I too in my timid youth. Coming and going like migratory birds. Then address the swallows fluttering in their dream like circles. Speak of the variety of circumstances that bring together such concords of men. Each man more than himself through whom an unknown life speaks. A circle ever returning into itself.'

aged woman ... her house Lady Gregory (1852–1932). See 'The New Faces'

western Coole Park is in County Galway, near the west, Atlantic coast

Hyde Douglas Hyde (1860–1949), poet, translator and scholar, learned Irish as a boy at Frenchpark, County Roscommon, where his father was

rector of Tibohine. Educated at Trinity College, Dublin, he founded the
Gaelic League in 1893, and became the first President of Ireland
(1938–45). Yeats praised his work in reviews and wrote a balanced
assessment of him in Dramatis Personae, *Autobiographies*, pp. 435–40
the Muses (Greek mythology) patronesses of art and science
one that ruffled ... pose Yeats himself who adopted a 'mask' of distant
polished pose and courtesy to hide his shyness
that slow man ... Synge John Millington Synge. See 'In Memory of Major
Robert Gregory'
Shawe-Taylor ... Lane Lady Gregory's nephews. John Shawe-Taylor
(1866–1911) brought about the settlement of the Land Question by
calling a conference (see Yeats's *Essays and Introductions*, pp. 343–5)
at a crucial moment. For Lane see 'To a Wealthy Man ... Pictures' and 'To a
Shade'
came ... swallows went swallows spend the summer in Ireland, then fly to
warmer climates in the autumn, returning in the spring
a compass-point swallows often fly round a turning point such as a steeple
or a high building
withershins the wrong or unexpected way, or a direction opposite the
apparent course of the sun
rooms and passages are gone the Forestry Department took over the estate
from Lady Gregory; she rented the house from the Department. When she
died the Department sold the house and the purchaser pulled it down,
largely for the value of the lead in the roof
laurelled head Lady Gregory. Poets in Greece were presented with
laurels

COOLE PARK AND BALLYLEE 1931   1931
(See Extended Commentaries – Text 6)

SWIFT S EPITAPH*   1930
A translation of the Latin epitaph Swift wrote for himself

The epitaph is in St Patrick's Cathedral, Dublin, of which Swift
was Dean, and where he is buried.

BYZANTIUM 1930

The poet imagines the afterlife in the golden city of Byzantium

The draft ran: 'Subject for a poem. Death of a friend Describe Byzantium as it is in the system [*A Vision*] towards the end of the first Christian millennium. A walking mummy. Flames at the street corners where the soul is purified, birds of hammered gold singing in the golden trees, in the harbour offering their backs to the wailing dead that they may carry them to Paradise'.

The poem should be read in conjunction with 'Sailing to Byzantium' (see notes on it). In an essay 'Modern Ireland', published posthumously in the *Massachusetts Review*, Winter 1964, Yeats described the Byzantium of his later poems as an example of magnificence, 'that city where the Saints showed their wasted forms upon a background of gold mosaic, and an artificial bird sang upon a tree of gold in the presence of the Emperor; and in one poem I have pictured the ghosts swimming, mounted upon dolphins, through the sensual seas, that they may dance upon its pavements'.

gong in one of Yeats's sources, W.G. Holmes, *The Age of Justinian and Theodora*, he pencilled 'Gong' opposite a description of the 'sonorous board suspended in each porch of each church, and beaten with mallets by a deacon'. The sea of the last stanza is 'gong-tormented' possibly because the sea is sensual (endowed with sensations and feelings), and the gong reminds its hearers of death

an image Yeats elsewhere alluded to 'the worldwide belief that the dead dream back' through the thoughts and deeds of their lives. The shade (ghost) fades out at last, but the spiritual being passes on to other states of existence

Hades' bobbin (Greek mythology) Hades or Pluto was lord of the underworld. This was probably a soul or spirit; the image may come from the Greek philosopher Plato's myth of Er in his *Republic* (S610)

A mouth ... breath a ghost, which can seem to live backwards through its past existence

Miracle, bird ... handiwork see the artificial bird of 'Sailing to Byzantium'

Emperor's pavement an open space, the Forum (known as the Pavement because of its marble floor) at Constantinople

blood-begotten spirits ghosts of human beings

leave after purgation

the dolphin's mire and blood (Greek mythology) dolphins carried the souls of the dead to the Islands of the Blest; Yeats read about this in Mrs Strong, *Apotheosis and the After Life* (1915)

VACILLATION 1931–2

The poet explores the idea of contraries, amidst the beauty of an autumn evening

Yeats met this idea in editing William Blake, and possibly in reading the German mystic Jakob Boehme (1575–1624). Yeats described the poem, in a letter to Mrs Shakespear written in November 1931, as a poor shadow of exciting experiences he had during two successive nights while walking after dark: the 'Autumnal image, remote, incredibly spiritual, erect delicate featured, and mixed with it the violent physical image, the black mass of Eden'.

antinomies contradictions (between conclusions which seem equally valid, necessary or reasonable)

A tree it is described in *The Mabinogion* (1838–49), a collection of Welsh legends

he that Attis' image hangs Attis was a vegetation god who castrated himself when his mother Cybele, the earth mother, drove him to frenzy, and 'he' is presumably one of his priests: his devotees castrated themselves at the March festival of the God, during which the priest used to hang the God's image on the sacred pine-tree

ram them an image Yeats took from Ben Jonson's *Poetaster*

Lethean foliage (Greek mythology) Lethe (oblivion) was a river in Hades, the underworld, and those who drank its water, souls about to be reincarnated, forgot their past lives

fortieth winter Yeats was forty in 1905; he may be thinking of the break-up of Maud Gonne's marriage in that year, and the 'Lethean foliage' may refer to his love for her which made him forget everything else

fiftieth year this experience of happiness (of 1915–16) is also described in prose, in Yeats's 'Anima Mundi', *Mythologies*, pp. 364–5

Responsibility Yeats felt a responsibility for his contribution to the thinking of modern Ireland and he thought back to the riots of 1897. See his *Autobiographies*, p. 368, and the poem 'The Man and the Echo' for 'Things said or done'

Chou probably Chou-Kung, of the twelfth-century Chinese Chou dynasty

Babylon the capital of Mesopotamia, famous for astronomy and astrology; the Babylonian Empire lasted from c.2200–538BC

Nineveh capital of the Assyrian Empire, destroyed by the Medes and Babylonians in 612BC

Isaiah's coal a reference to Isaiah 6:6–7: 'Then flew one of the seraphims unto me, having a live coal in his hand which he had taken with the tongs from off the altar; and he laid it upon my mouth and said, Lo this hath touched thy lips, and thine iniquity is taken away and thy sin purged'

Von Hugel Baron Friedrich von Hugel (1852–1925). Yeats had been reading his *The Mystical Element in Religion as Studies in St Catherine of Genoa and her Friends* (1908)

Saint Teresa ... Eternalised ... mummy St Teresa or Theresa of Avila (1515–82), a Spanish Carmelite nun. She wrote several books, including *The Way of Perfection*, *The Book of the Foundations* and *The Interior Castle*. Yeats wrote to Mrs Shakespear about this poem on 3 January 1932: 'I accept all the miracles. Why should not the old embalmers come back as ghosts and bestow upon the saint all the care once bestowed upon Rameses'

the lion and the honeycomb Yeats is thinking of Judges 14:5–18. Sampson killed a lion, in whose carcase bees made honey. He made a riddle out of this ('out of the strong came forth sweetness') but his Philistine wife pressed him till she got the answer and revealed it to his enemies

from WORDS FOR MUSIC PERHAPS (1932)

Published separately 1932, then included in *The Winding Stair and Other Poems* (1933).

'For Music' was just a name for these poems, Yeats told Mrs Shakespear; no-one would sing them. Crazy Jane was a character modelled upon 'Cracked Mary', an old woman who lived near Gort, County Galway, who was 'the local satirist' and had 'an amazing power of audacious speech'. The poems (written between 1926 and 1931) were intended to be 'all emotion and all impersonal … all praise of joyous life'.

CRAZY JANE ON GOD   1931

The passing nature of love and the permanence of God's knowledge

Banners … pass a reference to the idea that past actions can be re-enacted. See Yeats, *Mythologies*, p. 358

a house probably a reference to an Irish countrywoman seeing the ruined castle (Castle Dargan, near Sligo) lit up. See Yeats's *Explorations*, p. 369, *Autobiographies*, pp. 53 and 77, and his play *Purgatory* as well as notes on 'The Curse of Cromwell'

CRAZY JANE GROWN OLD LOOKS AT THE DANCERS   1929

A dream in which two lovers look as though they are about to kill each other

This records a dream Yeats had. He wrote to Mrs Shakespear describing how 'The man was swinging around his head a weight at the end of a rope or leather thong and I knew that he did not know whether he could strike her dead or not, and both sang their love for one another. I suppose it was Blake's old thought, "sexual love is founded on spiritual hate"'.

thraneen (Irish) a wisp of grass or hay. The phrase means 'not to care'

LULLABY*   1929

A mother sings her child to sleep

Paris one of the sons of Priam, king of Troy, who brought Helen, wife of Menelaus, King of Sparta, back to Troy with him, thus causing the Trojan War (here the 'world's alarms', perhaps)

Tristram … potion's work in the *Morte d'Arthur*, by Sir Thomas Malory (d. 1471), Tristram, son of the King of Lyonesse, falls in love with La Beale Isoud, daughter of the King of Ireland. He kills a brother of the Queen of

Ireland and returns to Cornwall, but King Mark sends him back to Ireland to arrange Isoud's marriage (to Mark). Tristram and Isoud drink a love potion unwittingly and fall irresistibly in love. They are betrayed to Mark, who eventually kills Tristram. In another version of the story Tristram sends for La Beale Isoud when he is dying in Brittany; she is to come in a ship with a white sail. He is told (by another Isoud) that the sail is black, and dies. La Beale Isoud discovers his body and dies beside it

Eurotas grassy bank the main river in Sparta, in which Leda was bathing when Zeus saw her

the holy bird ... Leda Zeus in the form of a swan. See 'Leda and the Swan'

AFTER LONG SILENCE 1929

In old age it is right to be friendly again after an affair in youth

This is written about Yeats and Mrs Shakespear, with whom he had an affair in 1896.

MAD AS THE MIST AND SNOW* 1929

The poet considers whether great genius is mad

Yeats had been ill, and could no longer spend his time 'amid masterpieces and trying to make the like' and 'gave part of every day to mere entertainment'. See *Explorations*, p. 436.

Horace Roman poet Quintus Horatius Flaccus (65–8BC)

Homer Greek epic poet (?b. between 1050–850BC), author of the *Iliad* and the *Odyssey*

Plato Greek philosopher, a pupil of Socrates at Athens; he taught there, then in Megara and Sicily, returning to teach in the Academy at Athens in 386BC

Tully's open page ... Cicero the Roman orator, author and politician, Marcus Tullius Cicero (106–43BC)

I AM OF IRELAND* 1929

A lyric, possibly a dance song, which is placed in the mouth of an Irish girl

This poem is founded on a fragment of an English manuscript (dating between 1300 and 1350).

O LD TOM AGAIN* 1931

A complex meditation on human enterprise, on birth and death

The invented character Tom appeared in 'Tom the Lunatic' and 'Tom at Cruachan', two other poems of 1931. (Tom Fool, or Tom o'Bedlam was a name applied to inmates of Bedlam, a lunatic asylum in London, and King Lear's fool was called Tom).

T HE DELPHIC ORACLE UPON PLOTINUS 1931

The poet describes the Greek idea of Heaven

This poem is based on an oracle given to Amelius who consulted the famous oracle at Delphi to find out where the soul of Plotinus, the **Neoplatonic** philosopher, had gone after his death. Yeats had been reading Stephen MacKenna's translation of Plotinus, and this poem echoes a passage from the Neoplatonist Porphyry's life of Plotinus (whose pupil he had been).

Bland Rhadamanthus one of the judges of souls in the underworld, 'bland' presumably because he is welcoming Plotinus
Golden Race Aeacus, Minos and Rhadamanthus, judges of souls in the underworld; the latter two are described by Porphyry as 'great brethren of the golden race of Zeus'. They look dim to Plotinus, but had provided a shaft of light to guide him
Plato see 'Among School Children'
Minos he was a son of Zeus and Europa
stately Pythagoras the adjective used by MacKenna; for Pythagoras see 'Among School Children'

from A WOMAN YOUNG AND OLD*

C HOSEN* probably 1920

The narrator chooses the lot of love in the whirling zodiac

The poem may reflect Plato's myth of Er in which the souls of men and women in heaven choose the lots which represent their future destinies. The rhyme scheme follows that of John Donne's 'Nocturnal upon St Lucie's Day'.

the lot ... chosen see note on Plato's Spindle in 'His Bargain'
Zodiac through which the sun moves
the miraculous stream the Milky Way
wrote ... astrologer Ambrosius Theodosius Macrobius, a fifth-century Neoplatonist, in his comment on Cicero's *Scipio's Dream*
changed into a sphere the souls of man and woman are ascending through the Zodiac. The 'whirling' of stanza 1 has become a sphere at a point where the Milky Way crosses the Zodiac

HER VISION IN THE WOOD   1926

Persephone's vision of Adonis, killed by a boar

This poem is based upon the Greek legend of Adonis, a youth loved by Aphrodite, the goddess of love. He was killed by a boar, but restored to life by Persephone on condition he spent six months of the year with her, six with Aphrodite.

the beast presumably the wild boar
Quattrocento (Italian) fifteenth century
Mantegna's the Italian painter Andrea Mantegna (1431–1506) lived at Padua and later at Mantua
no fabulous symbol the body being carried in the litter is not a god or hero but her lover

from A FULL MOON IN MARCH   (1935)

PARNELL'S FUNERAL   1933

Yeats considers Parnell's death as a sacrifice accepted, indeed willed by the Irish

Great Comedian's tomb that of the popular Irish political leader, Daniel O'Connell (1775–1847) of whose **rhetoric** Yeats disapproved, thinking his humour vulgar and gregarious: he described him as a comedian in contrast to Parnell whom he saw as a tragedian. The tomb is in Glasnevin Cemetery, Dublin

a brighter star Maud Gonne told Yeats on the evening of Parnell's funeral of the star that fell as his body was lowered into the grave

the Cretan barb in his *Autobiographies* Yeats described seeing between sleeping and waking a vision of 'a galloping centaur and a moment later a naked woman of incredible beauty, standing upon a pedestal and shooting an arrow at a star'. He annotated this passage very fully. The woman, he said, 'was, it seems, the Mother-Goddess' pictured in Cretan coins of the fifth century BC

a beautiful seated boy ... pierced boy his sacrificial death **symbolised** the death and resurrection of the Tree-spirit or Apollo

image of a star he is linked with Yeats's vision

woman, the Great Mother imaging ... heart the priestess enacting the role of the Great Mother. Yeats's notes in *Autobiographies* refer to the Cretan Jupiter making an image of his son, placing the boy's heart in a hollowed-out part (corresponding to the location of the heart) of the figure

Sicilian coin in his note in *Autobiographies* Yeats cited G.F. Hill, *A Handbook of Greek and Roman coins*, p. 163

strangers ... Emmet, Fitzgerald, Tone Irish leaders of the past, see notes on 'September 1913'

Hysterica passio (Latin), from *King Lear* II.4.57: 'Hysterica passio, down, thou climbing sorrow', meaning violence or madness

this quarry Parnell. See notes on 'To A Shade'

rhyme rats hear probably refers to the poet Seanchan Torpest killing rats by rhyme in Gort, County Galway

de Valera Eamon de Valera (1882–1975), President of Ireland (1959–72); his sentence of death for taking part in the 1916 Rising having been commuted to life imprisonment, he later led the anti-Treaty (of 1922, which brought the Irish Free State into being) republicans in the civil war; he was President of the Fianna Fail party 1926–59

Cosgrave William T. Cosgrave (1880–1965), First President of the Executive Council of the Irish Free State (1922–32); leader of the Opposition 1932–44

O'Higgins see note on 'Death'

O'Duffy Eoin O'Duffy (1892–1944), the head of the Garda Siochána (police) in the Irish Free State until 1933, who became Director of the Blueshirts,

and a Brigadier General in the Spanish army in the Spanish Civil War to
which he brought a contingent of Blueshirts
Jonathan Swift see 'Blood and the Moon' and 'The Seven Sages'

from SUPERNATURAL SONGS

RIBH AT THE TOMB OF BAILE AND AILLINN   1939

A monk reads his prayers at the tomb of two legendary Irish lovers, Baile and Aillinn

Ribh is an invented character, an old hermit who is reading his
breviary at midnight upon the tomb of the long dead lovers of Irish
legend, Baile and Aillinn, on the anniversary of their death, for, as
Yeats wrote to Mrs Shakespear, on that night they are united above
the tomb, 'their embrace being not partial but a conflagration of the
whole body and so shedding the light he reads by'.

me Ribh
tonsured head shaven as a mark of dedication by a priest or monk
Baile and Aillinn ... apple and the yew Aengus, the Irish god of love, wished
the lovers to be happy in his land among the dead, so he told each the
other was dead and they died of broken hearts. They were then changed
into swans linked with a golden chain. Over Baile's grave grew a yew tree,
over Aillinn's a wild apple, and their love was told on boards of wood, made
of yew and apple. Yeats wrote of them in 'The Withering of the Boughs'
(c.1900) and in 'Baile and Aillinn' (1903)

THERE*   1934 or 1935

A description of perfection

'There' describes perfection, the rounding off, the shape of a sphere
which is, in *A Vision*'s language, 'sufficient to itself'.

RIBH CONSIDERS CHRISTIAN LOVE INSUFFICIENT   probably 1934

Hatred of God may bring the soul to God

Richard Ellmann in *The Identity of Yeats* (1954), p. 283, suggests
that the poem arose from Mrs Yeats's automatic writing when

A FULL MOON IN MARCH continued

Yeats recorded in a journal that a 'communicator' had 'said "hate God", we must hate all ideas concerning God that we possess, that if we did not absorption in God would be impossible. The soul has to enter some significant relationship with God even if this be one of hatred'.

from LAST POEMS   (1936–9)

THE GYRES   1936–9

The poet contemplates the ruin of civilisation and prophesies its rising again

This poem contemplates the ruin of civilisation, faces this bravely with the advice of Old Rocky Face to rejoice, and, finally, suggests that 'a kind of civilization now unfashionable' will arise again (as is indicated in *A Vision*'s use of the gyres to indicate the cyclical rise and fall of civilisation).

The Gyres see note on 'Demon and Beast'

Old Rocky Face presumably some wise old eccentric, possibly founded on Shelley's Ahasuerus, described by Yeats in *Autobiographies*, pp. 171–3, as 'Master of all human knowledge, hidden from human sight in some cavern on the Mediterranean shore'. In MS drafts he is 'Old cavern man', 'old rocky face' and 'wrinkled rocky face'

Empedocles Greek philosopher (*c*.490–430BC) who believed all things (four primitive independent elements, air, water, fire and earth) were either blended by love (or affinity) or separated by hate (or antipathy). He envisaged a development of the perfect out of the imperfect, and a periodical return of things to the elemental state

Hector ... Troy see 'The Phases of the Moon'

painted ... tombs probably the discoveries in Egyptian tombs

Those ... again this sentence is easier to understand if it is read thus: Those whom Rocky Face holds dear (lovers of horses and women) shall disinter the workman, noble and saint from marble of a broken sepulchre, or dark betwixt the polecat and the owl, or any rich, dark nothing, and all things then run on that unfashionable gyre again

LAPIS LAZULI   1936

Tragedy, individual and public, should be faced bravely

This links a piece of lapis lazuli, dating from the Ch'ien Lung period (1731–95), that was given to Yeats by Harry Clifton for his seventieth birthday, with his thought that tragedy, individual and public, should be faced, bravely, gaily, an idea he found in Nietzsche, though an early poem, 'A Faery Song', links age and gaiety.

hysterical women   they are obsessed by fear of the coming war

nothing drastic is done   to stop the aggression of the Fascists and Nazis

Zeppelin   a German rigid-framed airship (named after the aircraft designer, Graf von Zeppelin); Zeppelins bombed London in the 1914–18 war

King Billy bomb-balls   an echo of 'The Battle of the Boyne', an Irish **ballad**, King Billy is William of Orange, who defeated James II at the Battle of the Boyne in Ireland in 1690:

> King James has pitched his tent between
> The lines for to retire
> But King William threw his bomb-balls in
> And set them all on fire

Hamlet ... Lear ... Ophelia ... Cordelia   Hamlet and Ophelia are characters in Shakespeare's *Hamlet*, Lear and Cordelia in his *King Lear*. The two women are unlike the hysterical women of the first line

lines to weep   Yeats, being told of a heroine weeping at the final curtain of a play by Lady Gregory, thought this should never occur

Black out   the darkening of lights as a measure against air raids, but also the darkening of the stage in a play. A black out is also a temporary loss of memory or consciousness

blazing into the head   Yeats thought that Shakespearean heroes conveyed a sudden enlargement of vision, an ecstasy at the approach of death, and quoted Lady Gregory's saying: 'Tragedy must be a joy to the man who dies'. See his *Essays and Introductions*, pp. 522–3

drop-scenes   curtains let down between the acts of a play

It   tragedy wrought to its utmost

Callimachus   a late-fifth-century Greek sculptor who was known for his technical skill

lamp-chimney he made a golden lamp for the Erechtheum in Athens which is described in Pausanias, *Description of Greece* I, 26, 6–7
Two Chinamen this begins the description of the lapis lazuli which stood on a mantelpiece in Yeats's house

AN ACRE OF GRASS   1936

(See Extended Commentaries – Text 3)

WHAT THEN?   probably 1936

Having achieved everything he set out to achieve, the poet, in old age, asks 'What then?'

This poem, like 'An Acre of Grass', was stimulated by a rereading of Nietzsche.

school The High School, Dublin, an Erasmus Smith foundation which Yeats attended 1881–3. He was earlier a pupil at the Godolphin School, Hammersmith, London 1875–80
Plato's ghost see 'The Tower', I
small old house Riversdale, Rathfarnham; see 'An Acre of Grass'

BEAUTIFUL LOFTY THINGS   probably 1937

Yeats remembers the nobility of his friends

This consists of particular moments of memory in which the nature of the people Yeats is remembering is recaptured. They seem to him, looking back, to have been like the Olympian gods and goddesses, superior to the mundane.

O'Leary's noble head see 'September 1913'
My father ... Abbey stage the artist John Butler Yeats (1839–1922) who spoke at the debate in the Abbey Theatre, Dublin, held after the riots which greeted Synge's *Playboy of the Western World* in 1907
Standish O'Grady ... drunken audience O'Grady (1846–1928), an Irish novelist and historian, whose writings had a great influence on Yeats and his generation. This prophetic speech on the future destiny of Ireland was delivered at a dinner in honour of the Irish Literary Theatre
Augusta Gregory ... drawn up see 'The New Faces', 'Coole Park, 1929' and 'Coole Park and Ballylee, 1931'. She told a threatening tenant who wanted

to take over some Coole Park land in the period of the Civil War 'how easy'
it would be to shoot her 'through the unshuttered window if he wanted to
use violence' when she wrote letters every evening
Maud Gonne Yeats first proposed to her at Howth in 1891; this is the only
time she is named in one of his poems
Pallas Athene he compared her to a goddess on many occasions
Olympians the Greek gods, who lived on Mount Olympus

THE CURSE OF CROMWELL*   probably 1936–7

A reflection on the ruin Cromwell brought to Ireland

This is meant to be spoken by a wandering peasant poet in Ireland,
and reflects the loss of an older civilisation crushed by Cromwell's
conquest and brutal treatment of it.

Cromwell's after Charles I was executed in 1649 and the Commonwealth
established, Oliver Cromwell (1599–1658) went to Ireland where he sacked
Drogheda and Wexford; he left in 1650 and confiscated very large amounts
of Irish land to be settled by Cromwellians
beaten into the clay this phrase comes from Frank O'Connor's translation
'Kilcash'. By the settlement Act of 1652 and a further act of 1653
Cromwell confiscated about 11 million out of the total of 20 million acres
of Irish land, leaving Irish landowners only Connaught and Clare, hence the
phrase 'to Hell or Connaught'
his fathers ... crucified a line from a translation of a poem by the Irish poet
Egan O'Rahilly (1670–1726)
fox ... Spartan boy's a story in the Life of Lycurgus (*c.*390–*c.*325BC) in the
Lives of the Ten Orators by Plutarch (*c.*AD46–120) tells how a Spartan boy
stole a fox and when caught hid it under his clothes: he let it gnaw him to
death rather than be found out to be a thief
great house ... old ruin see 'Crazy Jane on God'

THE WILD OLD WICKED MAN*   probably 1937–8

The old man prefers to think of the love of a woman rather than of God's power

The 'old man' in the skies is God. This is an old man's self-praise
and plea for love; when the woman says her love is for the old

man in the skies, the old man **persona** agrees that he has more experience, wit and knowledge than younger men and finds oblivion or escape from reality lying upon a woman's breast.

THE PILGRIM* 1937

The narrator scoffs at the pilgrims of Lough Derg

Possibly written after Yeats visited the Municipal Gallery in August: there is a painting of the Pilgrimage there which he recorded seeing on that visit. It deals with the pilgrimage to Lough Derg, a small lake on the borders of County Donegal and County Fermanagh.

Lough Derg's holy island St Patrick is supposed to have fasted in the cave on the island, and had a vision of the next world there. There are medieval accounts of the pilgrimage and Yeats read the Spanish dramatist Calderon's (1600–81) play on the subject, the Irish novelist William Carleton's (1794–1869) account of the pilgrimage and Archdeacon Seymour's *St Patrick's Purgatory: A Medieval Pilgrimage in Ireland* (1919)

the Stations of the Cross, usually fourteen: they depict Christ's passion and crucifixion

Purgatory where the Soul is purified, in Catholic doctrine, before going to heaven

black ... bird probably a bird described in an account by Antonio Mannini, a Florentine merchant who visited the purgatory in 1411, quoted by Archdeacon Seymour, *St Patrick's Purgatory*, pp. 55–7

THE MUNICIPAL GALLERY REVISITED 1937

An emotional visit to an art gallery which brings back many memories

This was prompted by a visit Yeats made to the Dublin Municipal Gallery in Charlemont Square, Dublin in August 1937. 'Restored to many friends' he sat down 'after a few minutes, overcome by emotion'.

thirty years he thought the pictures presented Ireland 'in spiritual freedom' and the pictures he mentions go back to the 1916 Rising, which could be taken as the creation of that freedom

An ambush probably a painting by Sean Keating (1889–1977)

pilgrims in *St Patrick's Purgatory* by Sir John Lavery (1856– 1941)

Casement in *The Court of Criminal Appeal* by Sir John Lavery. Sir Roger Casement (1864–1916) was a British consular official. He joined Sinn Fein in 1914, went to Germany, returned to Ireland in a U-boat in 1916 and was arrested in south-west Ireland; he was tried on a charge of high treason in London and hanged

Griffith Arthur Griffith (1872–1922) edited the *United Irishman* and *Sinn Fein*. Vice-president of Dail Eireann in 1918, he led the Irish plenipotentiaries who negotiated the Anglo-Irish treaty in 1921, became President of the Dail in 1922 and died that year

Kevin O'Higgins see 'Death'

revolutionary Soldier ... Tricolour in Lavery's painting *The Blessing of the Colours*; the soldier was a member of the Irish Free State army. The Irish flag is a tricolour with vertical stripes of green, white and orange: it echoes the pattern of the French flag adopted in the Revolution (which has stripes of blue, white and red)

woman's portrait possibly a portrait of Lady Beresford by the American painter John Singer Sargent (1856–1925) who worked in England from 1885

Heart-smitten ... recovering Yeats's heart was giving him trouble at the time of the visit

Augusta Gregory's son see 'In Memory of Major Robert Gregory'

her sister's son the portrait is by Charles Shannon (1863–1937), an English painter and lithographer and friend of Yeats

Hugh Lane see 'To a wealthy Man ... Pictures'. The portrait is probably that painted by Sargent

'onlie begetter' the phrase used in the dedication to 'Mr W.H.' in the Dedication to Shakespeare's *Sonnets*

Hazel Lavery Sir John Lavery's second wife (d. 1935) whose portrait was on Irish bank notes until recently

living and dying the first painting is *Hazel Lavery at her Easel*, the second *The Unfinished Harmony*

Mancini's portrait Antonio Mancini (1852–1930) Italian artist

Augusta Gregory see 'The New Faces', 'Coole Park, 1929' and 'Coole Park and Ballylee, 1931'

Rembrandt the famous Dutch painter and etcher Rembrandt van Rijn (1606–69)

John Synge see 'In Memory of Major Robert Gregory'

that woman ... that household Lady Gregory and Coole Park

Childless Yeats's first child, Anne Butler Yeats, was born in 1919

No fox ... Spenser an echo of Edmund Spenser's (?1552–99) 'The Death of
the Earl of Leicester': 'He now is gone, the whiles the Foxe is crept / Into
the hole, the which the badger swept'

Anteus-like Antaeus, son of Poseidon (god of the sea and the underworld in
Greek mythology), when attacked by Hercules, got strength from his mother,
Earth, whenever he touched the ground

noble and beggar-man Lady Gregory used to quote Aristotle: 'To think like a
wise man, but express oneself like the common people'. Lady Gregory and
Synge – and Yeats in some of his plays – made use of country people's
speech, dialect or Hiberno-English

ARE YOU CONTENT?   probably 1937 or 1938

As an old man, the poet laments that he is not content

The poem could be read as an answer to 'Introductory Rhymes' of
Responsibilities in which Yeats had lamented that he had no child,
only 'a book' to link him to his ancestors (see notes on various
ancestors there). His subsequent marriage in 1917 had continued
his family line; but he is still not content when he views his
achievement. This poem could also be compared with 'An Acre of
Grass' or 'The Man and the Echo'. The title, Timothy Webb
suggests, may derive from Shelley meeting a figure of himself at
Lerici which asked him how long he meant to be content. In
another version of this, a cloaked figure asked him in Italian, '*Siste
soddisfatto?*'

son his father John Butler Yeats; see 'Beautiful Lofty Things'

Grandson either the Rev. William Butler Yeats, the 'red-headed rector', or
'Old William Pollexfen', both mentioned in the second stanza

great-grandson most likely the Rev. John Yeats, described in the first two
lines of the second stanza; or William Pollexfen's father (details of whom
are not known) or William Middleton, the 'smuggler' of the second stanza
or, least likely, William Corbet (1737–1824)

He ... cross Rev. John Yeats, rector of Drumcliff, County Sligo. The cross is
Celtic in form and stands in Drumcliff churchyard

Sandymount Corbets Yeats's great-uncle Robert Corbet owned Sandymount Castle, south of Dublin. Yeats's father spent a lot of time there when he was an undergraduate and Yeats was born in a house nearby in 1865
Butlers far back a reference to the wife of Benjamin Yeats
Browning meant a reference to 'Pauline' (1833) by Robert Browning (1812–89): 'an old hunter / Talking with gods, or a high-crested chief / Sailing with troops of friends to Tenedos'

THE STATUES   1938

The poet writes about the influence of art or literature on civilisation

Pythagoras Yeats is suggesting that Pythagoras (see 'Among School Children') with his theory of numbers affected Greek sculptors who carved their statues by exact measurements
Greater than Pythagoras the Greek sculptors, not the Greek galleys that defeated the Persians at the naval battle of Salamis (480BC), really created Europe. In *On the Boiler* (1939) Yeats wrote that when 'the Doric Studios sent out those broad-backed marble statues against the multiform, vague, expressive Asiatic sea, they gave to the sexual instinct of Europe its goal, its fixed type'
Phidias the greatest sculptor of Greece (b. *c.*500BC), who was commissioned by Pericles to execute the main statues which were to adorn Athens; he built the Parthenon, the Propylaea, and himself carved the famous statue of the Athena at Athens and that of Zeus at Olympia
One image ... tropic shade Yeats is here referring to the effect of the Greek sculptors who followed Alexander the Great to India
No Hamlet ... Middle Ages the later image in this stanza of Grimalkin, a name for a cat (see Shakespeare's *Macbeth*, I.1.9), may have suggested the common notion that cats grow thin by eating flies, which was then transferred to *Hamlet*. The 'dreamer of the Middle Ages' appears in a passage in *Autobiographies* (pp. 141–2) which throws light on this elliptic stanza: 'the broad vigorous body suggests a mind that has no need of the intellect to remain sane, though it give itself to every fantasy: the dreamer of the Middle Ages. It is the resolute European image that yet half remembers Buddha's motionless meditation, and has no trait in common

with the wavering lean image of hungry speculation, that cannot but because of certain famous Hamlets of our stage fill the mind's eye. Shakespeare himself foreshadowed a symbolic change, that is a change in the whole temperament of the world, for though he called his Hamlet 'fat' and even "scant of breath", he thrust between his fingers agile rapier and dagger'

Empty eyeballs in *A Vision* Yeats wrote that the 'Greeks painted the eyes of marble statues and made out of enamel or glass or precious stones those of their bronze statues, but the Roman was the first to drill a round hole to represent the pupil, and because, as I think, of a preoccupation with the glance characteristic of a civilisation in its final phase'

grimalkin a cat, usually an old she-cat

Pearse summoned Cuchulain ... Post Office for Pearse see 'Easter 1916'. Yeats remarked in a letter (25 June 1938 to Edith Shackleton Heald) that 'Pearse and some of his followers had a cult' of Cuchulain the Irish hero (Pearse was in the General Post Office in Dublin, in front of which he read the proclamation of the Irish Republic in 1916; the building was heavily shelled, and Pearse and the others who had occupied it eventually surrendered); he continued: 'The Government has put a statue of Cuchulain [by Oliver Sheppard] in the rebuilt post office to commemorate this'

What intellect ... measurement ... face Pearse is described as summoning the forces of the past into being through the images created by intellect; the Cuchulain of the Irish legends, recreated through the literary revival, is given its archaic strength by contrast with the shapelessness of modern life, its 'formless spawning fury'

NEWS FOR THE DELPHIC ORACLE   1938

An ironic description of Poussin's *Marriage of Peleus and Thetis*

This is, in its contemplations of eternity, an **ironic** way of presenting earlier subjects and **imagery**. The fairy princess Niamh, treated idealistically in Yeats's early long poem *The Wanderings of Oisin* (1889), is now summed up as a 'Man-picker'. The great dead, the immortals, are seen as golden codgers. The whole poem has an earthy vigour about it; the dolphins conveying the souls 'pitch their burdens off; the last stanza describes a Poussin picture in earthy terms. Contrast this poem with 'The Delphic Oracle upon Plotinus'.

codgers a word usually used with derisive meaning for an old or eccentric man

Oisin the son of Finn and Saeve (of the Sidhe), he spent 300 years in three islands with Niamh in the other world in Yeats's *The Wanderings of Oisin*, which was founded on 'the Middle Irish dialogues of S. Patrick and Oisin and a certain Gaelic poem of the last century'

Pythagoras ... choir of love see 'Among School Children'

a dolphin's back see notes on dolphins in 'Byzantium'

Innocents possibly the Holy Innocents, children whom Herod's soldiers killed when Herod tried to eliminate Jesus. See Matthew 2:16–18

Peleus ... Thetis the stanza describes *The Marriage of Peleus and Thetis* (now entitled *Acis and Galatea*) by the French painter Caspar Poussin (1613–75) in the National Gallery of Ireland. In Greek legend Peleus married Thetis, a Nereid

Pan's cavern ... music Greek god of fertility, usually represented with horns on his human head, with the body of a goat from the waist down. He invented the flute and liked caverns

nymphs ... satyrs beautiful female nature spirits; ugly often goat-like sylvan gods who chased the nymphs

LONG-LEGGED FLY   1937–8

The need for silence at crucial moments in history

It concentrates upon the need for silence at crucial moments: when Caesar is making decisions affecting the future of civilisation, when Helen of Troy, believing herself unobserved, is dancing, when Michelangelo is painting the Sistine Chapel.

Caesar Caius Julius Caesar (?102–44BC) Roman general, statesman and historian

topless towers of Troy. The phrase comes from Christopher Marlowe's *The Tragical History of Dr Faustus*

She Maud Gonne

the Pope's chapel the Sistine Chapel in the Vatican, Rome

Michael Angelo who painted the famous ceiling in the chapel which shows Adam about to be awakened into life by God

HIGH TALK   1938

The circus stiltwalker becomes an extended metaphor

This is probably founded on memories of circuses visiting Sligo in Yeats's youth. Compare it with 'The Circus Animals' Desertion'. The stilts may refer back to the 'stilted boys', the old Irish heroes of 'The Circus Animals' Desertion'; their being stolen may refer to those who adopted Yeats's **Celtic Twilight** style, as in the poem 'A Coat'. Malachi is replacing the stolen stilts, but is stalking out of the town in the cold reality of dawn light, possibly the facing of death. Malachi may be based on the character of Oliver St John Gogarty (1878–1957), Yeats's friend, a successful Dublin surgeon, fellow Senator, poet, wit and autobiographer.

patching old heels the women are patching socks in upstairs rooms
Malachi Stilt-Jack Malachi is used as a Christian name, after the minor Hebrew prophet
sea-horses the waves

WHY SHOULD NOT OLD MEN BE MAD?   1936

Old age's disillusion with dreams of youth

This poem appeared in *On the Boiler* (1939), a prose work the title of which was owed to Yeats's memory of a mad ship's carpenter in Sligo, who denounced his neighbours – and general wickedness from a rusty old boiler. Here Yeats considers how people's lives turn out very differently from what might have been expected, how old men realise that no-one finishes life fully happy, fully worthy of the start they made; and that realisation seems an ample reason for old men being mad.

journalist probably R.M. Smylie, editor of the *Irish Times* at the time; like Yeats he had Sligo connections, his father having edited a Sligo newspaper
A girl Iseult Gonne

a dunce Francis Stuart (b. 1902), the novelist and poet, about whom Yeats had changing views. Stuart's *Black List* section H (1971) gives one account of the marriage

A Helen either Maud Gonne or Constance Markievicz (see 'In Memory of Eva Gore-Booth and Con Markiewicz')

THE CIRCUS ANIMALS' DESERTION   probably 1937–9

An exploration of the nature of poetic imagination

The first section describes how the poet, seeking a theme, has to settle upon his own heart, his personal experience; the second enumerates some of the old themes that triggered off and filled his poems, while the third returns to the heart – and its foul rag-and-bone shop.

Winter and summer ... on show this emphasises the totality of Yeats's commitment to his art, since circuses used to work a half-year season of performances

Stilted boys ... chariot ... Lion ... woman possibly the recreation of Irish legendary heroes such as Conchubar, Cuchulain, Fergus, Oisin and so on; the chariot may be Cuchulain's; the lion and woman may refer to Maud Gonne (described as 'half-lion half child' in 'Against Unworthy Praise', a poem included in *The Green Helmet and Other Poems* (1910)

sea-rider Oisin in Yeats's *The Wanderings of Oisin* he gallops off over the sea with Niamh

led by the nose Oisin and his friends when hunting meet Niamh on the edge of the sea, and she has chosen Oisin and has come to invite him to mount her horse with her, to know the Danaan leisure and have her as his wife

three enchanted islands, allegorical dreams they represent the three things man is always seeking, Yeats told his friend Katharine Tynan in a letter of 1888, 'infinite feeling, infinite battle and infinite repose' – summed up as gaiety, battle and repose in the poem

***Countess Cathleen* ... gave it** the play of this title which Yeats wrote for Maud Gonne, in which she played the Countess in the first production, 8 May 1899. In the play the Countess opposes two devils who offer to buy for gold the souls of starving peasants; she sacrifices her goods to buy food and sells her own soul, to the horror of the poet Kevin

my dear Maud Gonne
the Fool and Blind Man … sea this refers to the action of Yeats's play *On Baile's Strand* (1904). The Fool provides a commentary for the Blind Man while Cuchulain dies off stage fighting the waves
Heart-mysteries possibly a reference to Maud Gonne's marriage
the dream itself of an ideal love
Players and painted stage from 1903 to 1910 Yeats acted as General Manager of the Abbey Theatre

THE MAN AND THE ECHO 1938

The poet worries about the consequences of past actions; what happens after death is a mystery

This poem deals with death, and reaches the final admission that 'Man' simply does not know what may happen after death; he only knows that he hears the echo of his shouting to the Rocky Voice.

Alt a rocky fissure on Knocknarea, County Sligo
that play *Cathleen ni Houlihan* (1902), in which Maud Gonne played the part of Cathleen. The play had an impressive effect on its audiences. Yeats may have read Stephen Gwynn, *Irish Literature and Drama* (1936), p. 158. Gwynn attended the theatre but went home asking himself 'if such plays should be produced unless one was prepared for people to go out to shoot and be shot … Miss Gonne's impersonation had stirred the audience as I have never seen another audience stirred'
woman's reeling brain she was Margot Collis, who wrote under the name Margot Ruddock. Yeats wrote several poems about her: 'A Crazed Girl' of May 1936, 'Sweet Dancer' of January 1937, and 'Margot', published posthumously. There is an account of her madness in a letter of 22 May 1936 to Mrs Shakespear. See Yeats, *Letters* (1954), p. 856
a house possibly Coole Park, though it might imply 'big houses' in general
bodkin a symbol of suicide, a dagger or short sharp pointed weapon. The reference is to *Hamlet* III.1.76, in which Hamlet contemplates suicide; he 'might his Quietus make / With a bare bodkin'
Rocky Voice compare this image with that of 'Old Rocky Face' in 'The Gyres'
great night presumably of death

U NDER BEN BULBEN   1938

The poem suggests the reader should be in tune with occult wisdom, with the faery people who ride around Ben Bulben

This poem describes how a man has many incarnations. A fighting man briefly fulfils his soul's purpose, is decisive in his actions; this is something an artist can also achieve by putting men in touch with heaven. Now, because confusion reigns, Irishmen are urged to avoid their contemporaries, turning instead to the example of past traditions. The final stanza pictures the churchyard in County Sligo (where Yeats's body was reinterred – he died in France in 1939 – in 1948) with the poet's unconventional epitaph cut in a limestone gravestone.

sages ... Mareotic Lake see 'Demon and Beast'

Witch of Atlas in Shelley's poem 'The Witch of Atlas' she was a symbol of the beauty of wisdom, a Naiad turned into a cloud by the embrace of the sun. She travelled along the Nile 'by Moeris and the Mareotid Lakes'

those horsemen ... women probably the visionary people described to Yeats by his uncle George Pollexfen's maid Mary Battle. See notes on Pollexfen, 'In Memory of Major Robert Gregory'

Ben Bulben the mountain in Sligo particularly associated with the Fianna, the mounted warriors who served Finn

Mitchel John Mitchel (1815–75), an Irish nationalist. Transported to Australia, he wrote in November 1853 a powerful *Jail Journal* (1854) in which he, in parody of the Anglican order of Service 'Give us peace in our time, O Lord', substituted 'war' for 'peace'. He escaped from Australia to America, returning later to become an MP in Ireland

a stark Egyptian Plotinus, born in Lycopolis, Egypt, who thought objects were themselves imitations, and that art imitated objects, thus going back to the ideas from which Nature derives

gentler Phidias see 'The Statues'

Sistine Chapel ... Adam see 'Long-legged Fly'

Quattrocento (Italian) fifteenth century

Calvert Edward Calvert (1799–1883), visionary artist

Wilson Richard Wilson (1714–82), landscape painter

Blake William Blake, English poet, painter, engraver and mystic

Claude Claude Lorrain (1600–82), French landscape painter

Palmer's phrase Yeats in his essay 'Blake's illustrations to Dante' (*Essays and Introduction*, p. 125) quoted Samuel Palmer, who described Blake's illustrations (in Thornton's *Virgil*) to the first Eclogue as being 'like all this wonderful artist's work, the drawing aside of the fleshly curtain, and the glimpse which all the most holy studious saints and sages have enjoyed, of the rest which remains to the people of God' (a reference to Hebrews 4:9)

the lords and ladies … clay from Yeats's friend the Irish author Frank O'Connor's translation *Kilcash*: 'The earls, the lady, the people beaten into the clay'

Irishry term used by Edmund Burke to distinguish native Irish people from the Englishry, or English settlers in Ireland

Drumcliff churchyard and … An ancestor Yeats arranged that he should be buried in the churchyard where his great-grandfather had been rector, on the road to Bundoran to the north of Sligo in a valley lying at the foot of Ben Bulben. He died at Roquebrune, France on 28 January 1939; his body was reinterred at Drumcliff on 17 September 1948

PART THREE

CRITICAL APPROACHES

In reaching a critical estimate of Yeats's poems, as mentioned in How to Study a Poem, a good thing to do is to read a poem aloud, to get to know it, to be aware of its meaning or meanings (this may involve reading the notes in an annotated edition or commentary) before pondering what Yeats intended in writing it, and how far he succeeded in creating something lasting. Why lasting? That question is best answered by others. What is your test of a good poem? What makes you think well of it? Perhaps a readiness to reread it? To remember it?

Yeats uses **rhyme** and **scansion** to help his readers, to make his poems memorable: he uses literary devices; he is a master of **rhetoric**, the art of making words obey his call, in order to create the emotional as well as the intellectual reactions he seeks from his audience.

In assessing the success, or, perhaps, in your judgement, the failure of a poem, it may be worth considering its ability to arrest your attention through its phrasing, its **imagery**, its subject matter, its capacity to evoke a mood, to crystallise an idea, to challenge with a question. Does it explore a situation, convey the sense of an individual's delight, joy, misery, despair? Does that individual's experience spill over into a universal affirmation or questioning? Does Yeats's preoccupation with the personal, his rootedness in Irish literature, history and politics, his love of Irish scenery, his romantic idealism, his bitterness, or his sensuality transcend his immediate circumstances? Do his reactions to the nature of life in Ireland and in the world at large work in such a way that his words can still crystallise situations, can still deal with universal situations that go beyond his contemporary circumstances?

Do you find the complex interrelationships of his poems successful? Does the **symbolism** he built up over the years contrive to carry more than mere obvious meanings? Do you find more meaning in a poem when you return to it? Have you changed in your own attitudes, your own understanding? How far has the poet actually affected you in your responses?

THEMES

There are many, overlapping themes in Yeats's poetry. Often it is hard to decide into which category of theme one would place a poem.

IRISH MYTHOLOGY, NARRATIVE, CHARACTER AND PLACES

'Fergus and the Druid', 'Cuchulain's Fight with the Sea' and 'The Hosting of the Sidhe' are good examples of Irish mythology. Other poems treat Irish narrative themes; as they are necessarily long they are not included in full in the paperback selections. *The Wanderings of Oisin* is an obvious example. In *Collected Poems* and *Yeats's Poems* you will find 'The Old Age of Queen Maeve' and 'The Two Kings'. 'The Ballad of Moll Magee', 'The Lake Isle of Innisfree', 'The Fiddler of Dooney', 'Red Hanrahan's Song about Ireland', 'The Wild Swans at Coole', 'Coole Park, 1929' and 'Coole Park and Ballylee, 1931' are examples of poems about Irish character and places.

THE POET'S FAMILY

Other themes centre on Yeats's family, such as 'Introductory Rhymes', 'A Prayer for my Daughter' and 'Under Saturn'.

A VISION

There are themes which derive from the thought of *A Vision*. 'Ego Dominus Tuus', 'The Phases of the Moon', 'The Second Coming', 'Leda and the Swan', 'Sailing to Byzantium', 'Ribh considers Christian Love Insufficient', 'Lapis Lazuli' and 'The Gyres' are all connected with the theme of historical change and the human personality that Yeats treated in *A Vision*. He uses the symbol of the gyres to illustrate his ideas about an age being the opposite of an age, of contrariety and tension, while the phases of the moon allow him to discuss human types.

THE SUPERNATURAL

The supernatural provided Yeats with plenty of themes. 'The Stolen Child' is a good example of this **genre**, and 'The Man who Dreamed of

Faeryland' and 'The Host of the Air' are other early examples of Irish supernatural topics. 'The Mountain Tomb' reflects his Rosicrucian knowledge.

LOVE

Poems about love contain themes of praise and devotion as in the early 'Ephemera', 'The Pity of Love', 'The Sorrow of Love': these have a strain of mournfulness running through them. 'The White Birds' is wistful and sad. 'The Lover tells of the Rose in his Heart' and 'The Song of Wandering Aengus' have more optimism. See how you categorise such love poems as 'He Bids His Beloved be at Peace', 'He gives his Beloved Certain Rhymes' and 'He Remembers Forgotten Beauty'. The theme of offering the beloved his dreams reaches its height in 'He wishes for the Cloths of Heaven'. The theme changes to contemplation of change in love and the beloved with 'The Arrow' and 'Never Give all the Heart', while 'Words', 'Reconciliation' and 'No Second Troy' recognise the passing of love's exaltation and hopefulness. The poems of *Words for Music Perhaps* carry themes of physicality, Crazy Jane an exuberant, earthy figure in them, while those of *A Woman Young and Old* have a more intellectual content, the themes stressing the inevitability of love – as in 'Before the World was made' or 'Chosen'. There are themes illustrating moments of delight as in 'Parting' or 'A Last Confession'. The range, the variety of love themes, is worth pondering – a chronological approach may be rewarding in showing the development of the poet's attitudes to love.

AGE

Age occupied Yeats from early in his poetic career. There are the poems which play upon the themes of the detachment of old age in beggars or hermits ('The Three Hermits', 'Beggar to Beggar Cried'); there are poems which are more personal and some which rage about the infirmity of old age ('The Wild Old Wicked Man', 'Are You Content?' or 'Why should not Old Men be Mad?'). The feeling of frustration emerges in 'Are You Content?', the knowledge that he will never know what happens after life in 'The Man and the Echo' and 'What Then?'

POLITICS

Politics produce angry themes, contrasting the mean and the generous, those with vision and the philistines. The political note is stressed in 'Upon a House Shaken by the Land Agitation', 'To a Wealthy Man ...', 'September 1913' and 'To a Shade' where the theme of denunciation, scorn and anger prevails. The theme of violence emerges in many poems, such as 'Meditations in Time of Civil War' and 'Nineteen Hundred and Nineteen' or 'Blood and the Moon'. In old age 'The Curse of Cromwell' and 'Parnell's Funeral' show Yeats's themes of bitterness in different forms, though his final use of the theme in 'Politics' rejects the importance of politics in favour of love and beauty.

THE ART OF POETRY

Poetry itself is a general theme he employed with vigour. 'All things can tempt me', 'The Coming of Wisdom with Time', 'A Coat' and 'The Fisherman' show us the difficulties he experienced, with inspiration, the fading of intensity, the shift in sensibility, the difference between ambition and reality. 'The Scholars' and 'The People' have as their respective themes the division between poetry and scholars, poet and the people. The theme of romance is the backbone of 'Coole and Ballylee, 1931', the question of inspiration, the contrast between the courtly show of the early poetry and the perhaps sordid sources of it, the theme of 'The Circus Animals' Desertion'.

There are many other themes to consider: among them are those of dreams, of friendship, of mood, or grotesqueries, of Indian or Arcadian poetry, of adaptations and translations. When you read a poem you may find it rewarding to pick out the main theme and consider how Yeats counterpoints it with others, or how he will repeat a theme but vary it sufficiently to create a new dimension, a new slant upon his subject. Remember, too, that he uses many themes drawn from classical literature and from English poets from Chaucer through Shakespeare to the Romantics and Victorians.

Yeats wrote well over 500 poems in the fifty-eight years that he was writing poetry: during those years he developed and changed his style, and, naturally enough, his use of imagery and language changed too. You may be surprised at the extent of his vocabulary if you have access to the *Concordance to the Poems of W.B. Yeats*, edited by Stephen M. Parrish and published in 1963.

In the early poetry the imagery is heroic, related to the Gaelic legends and to aspects of country folklore and life in Ireland; added to this is the imagery of the Rose which is used in love poetry but also suggests Rosicrucian and occult symbolism. The latter imagery can hardly have conveyed Yeats's meanings fully to his contemporary readers. He did, however, learn from Shelley's repetition of symbols and we find in his poems repeated images of the sea, the river, the fountain, the shell, and then, in later poetry, caves, towers, the Mareotic lakes, rocks, thorn bushes, trees, woods *et cetera*.

As Yeats shifted from his **Celtic Twilight** poetry the language changed as well as the imagery; he shed the adjectives which tended to have a melancholic effect, such as sleepy, fretful, dim, pale, heavy, inarticulate, pendulous, waning, wandering, old, lame, dead, dewy, dreamy. (These adjectives come from just three early poems.)

Decoration demanded other adjectives such as golden and silver (as in 'The Man who dreamed of Faeryland') allied with sun and moon (as in 'The Song of Wandering Aengus'). There is a rich tapestry of varied imagery in some poems (as in 'He Remembers Forgotten Beauty') while the language is repeated (as in 'He Gives His Beloved Certain Rhymes' or 'He Wishes for the Cloths of Heaven'). By his middle and late period Yeats exhibits a mastery of repetition (particularly in the two Byzantine poems).

The imagery of places (and the legends associated with them) has a strong effect, sometimes (as in 'Red Hanrahan's Song about Ireland') with sound effects, sometimes (as in 'Under Ben Bulben') with visual ones. Similarly proper names, often repeated, carry resonances of meaning from other poems: thus Cuchulain, Fergus, Maeve, Hanrahan, Robartes, Aherne, Crazy Jane, or Parnell evoke responses from the reader who has come to know their significance.

The middle period had shed the earlier decorative imagery, something 'The Coming of Wisdom with Time' put very succinctly: the poet, now that the days of flowers and leaves are over may wither into truth, 'All Things Can Tempt Me' providing the strong wish to get rid of the language and imagery which were formerly so romantic.

New imagery drawn from his experience of Italy in 1907 began to enter the poems – Urbino and Ferrara and the rich achievement of Italian art. His reading continued, and there are classical images now which show that he is no longer concentrating upon Irish subjects: Catullus, Perseus, Empedocles, Hector, Helen, Oedipus, Paris, Leda, Plotinus, Pythagoras, Plato, to name but a few examples. And he uses the names of eighteenth-century Anglo-Irish writers to good effect: Burke, Berkeley, Goldsmith and Swift, each accompanied by suitable imagery.

Yeats's use of **rhetoric** developed. Repetition has been mentioned and his use of the question should also be considered. Good examples can be found in 'The Wild Swans at Coole', 'The Scholars', 'Among School Children' or 'What Then?'. The final question in a poem can be a virtual statement, an **ironic** twist, a confession of ignorance, or a heartfelt cry. Questions can set the scene, or make a comment, or pose a philosophical problem. You can find examples of these different usages in, say, 'Upon a House Shaken by the Land Agitation', 'The People', 'Michael Robartes and the Dancer'. 'Nineteen Hundred and Nineteen', 'The Tower II' or 'The Man and the Echo'. The variety of technique is indeed impressive.

PART FOUR

EXTENDED COMMENTARIES

Examples of Yeats's early, middle and late poetry will reveal how themes or images recur, how his style changes, and will show the particular achievement in each period.

TEXT 1   THE LAKE ISLE OF INNISFREE

I will arise and go now, and go to Innisfree,
And a small cabin build there, of clay and wattles made:
Nine bean-rows will I have there, a hive for the honey-bee,
And live alone in the bee-loud glade.

And I shall have some peace there, for peace comes dropping slow,
Dropping from the veils of the morning to where the cricket sings;
There midnight's all a glimmer, and noon a purple glow,
And evening full of the linnet's wings.

I will arise and go now, for always night and day
I hear lake water lapping with low sounds by the shore;
While I stand on the roadway, or on the pavements grey,
I hear it in the deep heart's core.

This early poem, the most anthologised of Yeats's poems (something which caused him some embarrassment in later life) was written in Bedford Park, the London suburb where the Yeatses lived from 1888. Yeats was twenty-three when he first wrote it and very homesick for Sligo. Walking through Fleet Street, he heard a tinkling of water coming from a shop 'where a little water jet balanced a wooden ball upon its point'. The sound suggested the lapping of lake water to him and out of his remembrance of Lough Gill in County Sligo came the poem. The final version appeared in the *National Observer* in December 1890, but he sent this early two-stanza version to his friend Katharine Tynan in a letter of December 1888, describing Innisfree (Heather Island in Irish) as a beautiful little rocky island in Lough Gill with a legended past. Comparing the early and the published versions shows what Yeats achieved in revising and rewriting. Here is the early version:

> I will arise and go now and go to the island of Inis free
> And live in a dwelling of wattles – of woven wattles and wood work made,
> Nine bean rows will I have there, a yellow hive for the honey bee
> And this old care shall fade
>
> There from the dawn above me peace will come down dropping slow
> Dropping from the veils of the morning to where the household cricket sings,
> And noontide there be all a glimmer, midnight be a purple glow,
> And evening full of the linnet's wings

He told her that in his story (the novel *John Sherman*, published in 1891) he had made one of the characters when in trouble long to go away and live alone on the island – an old daydream of his own. He had been influenced by hearing his father's reading aloud from the American author Henry Thoreau's *Walden* a description of how Thoreau had lived the simple life for two years in a cabin he built by Walden Pond, near Concord in Massachusetts. Katharine Tynan's poem 'Thoreau at Walden' probably also reminded him of this. Another input into the poem was his reading a *History of Sligo* (1882) with its story of a tree that bore berries, which were the food of the gods, growing upon Innisfree, guarded by a monster. A girl on the mainland, pining for the fruit, sent her lover to kill the monster and bring her the fruit. He did so, but died of tasting it. In sorrow or remorse she too ate it and died. In his *Autobiographies* (pp. 71–2) Yeats wasn't sure whether he chose to daydream about the island because of its beauty or because of the story. He added a note to another poem, 'The Danaan Quicken [the old Irish name for mountain ash or rowan] Tree' of 1893, explaining that the berries were the food of the Tuatha de Danaan or fairies.

So we have a daydream founded upon a dislike of living in London (though Yeats spent much of his life there, his poems don't ever allude to it directly) with its roadway and its pavements grey, upon his love of the Sligo countryside and its legends, and a strong escapist desire to live there in the self-sufficient way suggested by Walden.

There are two strong biblical echoes, and echoes often strengthen a poem and add to its effectiveness. The first line reminds us of the parable of the prodigal son in Luke 15:18 'I will arise and go to my father' and the ninth of the cleansing of the unclean spirits in Mark 5:5 'and always night and day, he was in the mountains'. The double repetition of 'and go' in the first and last stanza and of 'and' in the first, second and third stanzas, gives the poem a certain simplicity and deliberation, a repetitive echoing sound that suits the subject. The inversion arrests attention, while the repetition continues in the second stanza ' peace ... peace ... dropping ... dropping'; and in the third stanza the repetition of the first six words of the first adds to the suggestion of solemnity, almost of ritual; a similar effect comes from the repetition of 'for' in the second and third stanzas; the second use of it concentrates on the strength of the sound of the lake water remembered in the midst of the city, and the last line punches home the essence of the poem: the exile's awareness of what he loves. There is another key to the poem in that last line which emphasises his hearing the 'low sounds', for it is the sound quality, the verbal music of the whole poem that is so effectively achieved. The devices of **assonance** and **consonance** are brilliantly deployed, and the **alliteration** is as skilfully used as is the unobtrusive internal **rhyming**. Technically, then, this poem is a *tour de force*, with its subject having an immense appeal to the escapist element in most of us.

TEXT 2   NO SECOND TROY

Why should I blame her that she filled my days
With misery, or that she would of late
Have taught to ignorant men most violent ways,
Or hurled the little streets upon the great,
Had they but courage equal to desire?
What could have made her peaceful with a mind
That nobleness made simple as a fire,
With beauty like a tightened bow, a kind
That is not natural in an age like this,
Being high and solitary and most stern?

> Why, what could she have done, being what she is?
> Was there another Troy for her to burn?

In this middle-period poem, which headed a Diary entry and was dated December 1908, Yeats contemplates what Maud Gonne has meant to him. He had fallen in love with her at their first meeting in 1889; from then on he had written love poems to her (many of the most despairing ones are in *The Wind Among the Reeds* (1899)) and kept hoping to marry her. They had a spiritual marriage in 1898; they shared dreams and visions. He proposed to her yet again in 1899 and in 1901. A key poem, written in his progress towards a new style, 'Adam's Curse', recording a meeting with Maud in London, reveals something of his mood in 1902, an inability to maintain the 'old high way of love'. Nevertheless he was shattered by the news of her impending marriage to Major John MacBride (and in an agonised letter explained painfully and plainly his reasons against it; MacBride's family were also opposed to it. See *The Gonne-Yeats Letters* (1992) pp. 30–5) which took place in February 1903. The marriage did not survive for long; in February 1905 Maud sued for divorce in Paris on the grounds of MacBride's debauchery, adultery, drunkenness and other matters. She was granted a separation but not a divorce because of legal complications about MacBride's domicile. Maud continued to live in France.

'No Second Troy', a terse and compact poem, seems at first a long way from the romantic devotion of poems such as 'He wishes for the Cloths of Heaven' or the idealism of 'Red Hanrahan's Song about Ireland'. It begins reflectively, recording her effect on him, regrets her revolutionary activities, particularly her inciting the 'ignorant men' who, as Joseph Hone put it, formed little 'semi-literary and semi-political clubs out of which the Sinn Fein movement grew' and which Yeats distrusted. Yet he can admire her beauty, the nobleness of her mind, her seeming to belong to another world, an ancient civilisation – elsewhere he compared her to Pallas Athene, or saw her as an impersonation of the spring. Her high and solitary nature reminds him of a Greek statue. But then comes the ultimate tribute. Though there is now no question of marrying her, he can still praise her in the midst of his regrets and reservations. She is like Helen of Troy (whose carrying off by Paris caused the Trojan Wars), she is beyond comment, inevitable in her actions and their effects. The poem's conversational tone arises at first from the simplicity of the vocabulary, the absence of decoration – for every word counts. Her beauty being 'like a tightened bow' may owe something to Blake's symbolism and suggest her sexual attraction, but the bow also reminds us of the violence of revolution and warfare, and prepares us for the final image, the destruction of Troy by force, something brought about by a woman's beauty and sexual attraction. And Troy leads us, in what is a new kind of love poem, to the final statement, put in the form of apparently unanswerable questions.

See other poems likening Maud Gonne to Helen of Troy: 'A Woman Homer Sung', 'Peace' and 'When Helen Lived'.

TEXT 3 AN ACRE OF GRASS

Picture and book remain,
An acre of green grass
For air and exercise,
Now strength of body goes;
Midnight, an old house
Where nothing stirs but a mouse.

My temptation is quiet.
Here at life's end
Neither loose imagination,
Nor the mill of the mind
Consuming its rag and bone,
Can make the truth known.

Grant me an old man's frenzy,
Myself must I remake
Till I am Timon and Lear
Or that William Blake
Who beat upon the wall
Till Truth obeyed his call;

A mind Michael Angelo knew
That can pierce the clouds,

Or inspired by frenzy
Shake the dead in their shrouds;
Forgotten else by mankind,
An old man's eagle mind.

This late poem, written in November 1936, and inspired by rereading Nietzsche, especially *The Dawn of Day*, can be compared to a complementary poem, 'What Then?', first published in April 1937, but probably also written in 1936. Yeats was now into his seventies but his poetry was still vigorous and challenging. These two poems may suggest why.

The opening stanza of 'An Acre of Grass' sketches the scene with consummate, economical ease. Yeats and his family were now living in an old farmhouse, Riversdale, outside Rathfarnham, at the foot of the Dublin mountains. He wrote enthusiastically about it to his friend Mrs Shakespear in several letters; he enjoyed the trees in the old fruit garden, the flower garden, the pergolas covered with roses, the grass lawns. And once the familiar pictures were on the walls, the inside of the house delighted him as much as its grounds.

Curiously enough, this was the fulfilment of a dream; for in an essay of 1917 (*Mythologies* p. 342) he envisaged a poet growing old, discovering rhythms in the seasonal patterns like those of sleep, and so the poet would 'never awake out of vision'. But then he had remembered Wordsworth, 'withering into eighty years, honoured and empty-witted', and thought of climbing to some waste room to 'find, forgotten there by youth, some bitter crust'. He knows he is now at life's end and still does not know the truth. As usual this poem relates to other poems; the 'rag and bone' milled by the poet's mind suggests 'The Circus Animals' Desertion', another late poem which contemplates his early poetry and his toil for the theatre, and then, in a devastating final stanza, turns to what prompted all his work, 'the foul rag-and-bone shop of the heart'.

Unlike Wordsworth, Yeats demands for himself an old man's frenzy. In an arresting phrase, 'Myself must I remake', he links himself with fierce old men (no doubt remembering his fierce old Pollexfen grandfather), Timon, Lear and Blake. He seeks a mind like that of Michelangelo (a figure found elsewhere in late poems, notably in 'Under Ben Bulben' and, less directly, in 'Long-Legged Fly'). The poem develops; it moves from the 'truth' at the end of the second stanza that cannot be known by his loose imagination, or his going back over the past's rag and bone, to Blake's beating upon the wall in the third stanza to make Truth obey his call. The need for the frenzy that will impel the remade poet (who had earlier remade himself by dint of his ideas of adopting a mask) is emphasised again in the last stanza. Here the power of the mind, now an eagle mind able to soar or plunge at will (an echo of an early poem 'Upon a House Shaken by the Land Agitation'), can, ultimately, answer the vain questioning of the second stanza. The quiet established so skilfully in the first two stanzas (the old man's temptation is quiet, his strength of body is going; only a mouse is stirring) is now shattered by the repeated use of the noun 'frenzy' and the dynamic verbs 'remake'; 'beat'; 'pierce'; 'shake'. The poem has achieved a subtle counterpointing. The image of the mouse of the first stanza is replaced by that of an eagle. The word 'old' alters with its associations as the poem progresses. First it is applied simply and descriptively to the house, then to the old man. Unexpectedly, paradoxically even, he searches for, indeed demands enabling frenzy. Finally, once the limitations of age are overcome, its potential realised through the energetic remaking of the self, comes the triumphant achievement of an old man's eagle mind.

TEXT 4   SAILING TO BYZANTIUM

I

That is no country for old men. The young
In one another's arms, birds in the trees
– Those dying generations – at their song,
The salmon-falls, the mackerel-crowded seas,
Fish, flesh, or fowl, commend all summer long
Whatever is begotten, born, and dies.
Caught in that sensual music all neglect
Monuments of unageing intellect.

II

An aged man is but a paltry thing,
A tattered coat upon a stick, unless

Soul clap its hands and sing, and louder sing
For every tatter in its mortal dress,
Nor is there singing school but studying
Monuments of its own magnificence;
And therefore I have sailed the seas and come
To the holy city of Byzantium.

III

O sages standing in God's holy fire
As in the gold mosaic of a wall,
Come from the holy fire, perne in a gyre,
And be the singing-masters of my soul.
Consume my heart away; sick with desire
And fastened to a dying animal
It knows not what it is; and gather me
Into the artifice of eternity.

IV

Once out of nature I shall never take
My bodily form from any natural thing,
But such a form as Grecian goldsmiths make
Of hammered gold and gold enamelling
To keep a drowsy Emperor awake;
Or set upon a golden bough to sing
To lords and ladies of Byzantium
Of what is past, or passing, or to come.

This poem is typical of many of the poems of Yeats's maturity in
its treatment of the effects of old age, its attempts to remedy them
by contemplation of an idealised Byzantium. A companion poem
'Byzantium' was written in 1930. Yeats had read about Byzantium in
Edward Gibbon, *The Decline and Fall of the Roman Empire* (1776; 1781
and 1788), W.G. Holmes, *The Age of Justinian and Theodora* (1905) and
O.M. Dalton, *Byzantine Art and Archaeology* (1923). The symbolic
meaning he attached to the city was made clear in *A Vision* where he
selected the period in the city's history 'a little before Justinian opened St
Sophia and closed the Academy of Plato'; he thought that in that period
'religious, aesthetic and practical life, were one', that architect and
artificers (it was a great age of building in Byzantium) spoke to the

multitude and the few alike, that 'the painter, the mosaic worker, the worker in gold and silver, the illuminator of sacred books were almost unpersonal, almost perhaps without the consciousness of individual design, absorbed in their subject matter and that the vision of a whole people' (see *A Vision* (1937), pp. 279–80). Yeats had admired the magnificent mosaics with their frieze of virgins and martyrs at Ravenna during his visit to Italy in 1907; when recovering from illness in 1924 he had gone to Sicily where he saw the Byzantine mosaics at Monreale and Palermo. And he regarded Byzantium in the eighth century as the centre of European civilisation and the source of its spiritual philosophy, a city with a unified culture. He had put some of his thoughts about, in the Irish phrase, 'making his soul' (or preparing for death) into 'Sailing to Byzantium', symbolising the search for the spiritual by a voyage to that city.

Its oracular tone and unusual content are at first challenging – indeed an American critic once complained about the difficulty of assimilating all this magnificence at once. But if you read it through it falls into pattern. And pattern is emphasised in the structure of the poem's stanzas which are based on a stanza form used by Tasso and Ariosto among others, which consists of eight lines, usually eleven syllabled, with a rhyme scheme of *ababab cc*, **ottava rima**. Yeats does not always keep strictly to this rhyme, and some of his stanzas rhyme *ababacdd*. (Other poems, particularly in *The Tower* volume are also written in this form.) Does the fact that the sixth line is not rhymed in the first three stanzas but is in the fourth add to (or lessen) the impact of 'sing' in the fourth stanza?

As to its content: stanza I emphasises youth and physical vigour. (The poem was triggered off by the sixty-one-year-old poet seeing a pair of lovers in each other's arms. Enviously? Perhaps.)

The lovers are in the present. The present crowds in on the poet and on us with all its vibrating sensuality. Attention turns from the human lovers to the birds singing in the trees, generative yet dying generations. This is the contradiction, of death in life (and may well be an echo of the first anthem for the Burial of the Dead in *The Book of Common Prayer*: 'in the midst of life we are in death'). Other images evoke the vigour of creative life: the salmon leaping on their way upstream to spawn (their dynamic strength suggestive of the uncoiling power of the

Irish hero Cuchulain's salmon leap?); the mackerel teeming in profligate profusion around the Irish shores. 'Fish, flesh or fowl' – notice the powerful effect of the **alliteration** in this condensed emphatic recapturing of the salmon and mackerel, the fleshy human lovers, the fowls of the air (a biblical echo here) in the trees – commend all through the long summer, the season of physical heat, whatever is begotten in that heat, is born and dies. This is sensual music, the great chime of physical nature in which 'all neglect monuments of unageing intellect'. The emphatic sensual music reaches its peak in the neglect of intellectual achievements. We are being prepared for what is to come: its opposite.

John Donne, the seventeenth-century **metaphysical** poet, was a poet who emphasised apparent contradictions, and wrote of contraries: 'Oh, to vex me, contraries meet in one.' And William Blake, the late eighteenth-century poet proclaimed in *The Marriage of Heaven and Hell* that without contraries there is no progression. 'Attraction and Repulsion, Reason and Energy, Love and Hate are necessary to Human Experience.' Yeats, too, was attracted by the idea of contraries. In stanza II he introduces the soul, to counterbalance the preceding emphasis upon the sensual music, to make an aged man more than a paltry, a frail thing. But the poem is more than a matter of contraries: old and young have been contrasted from the start. It contains some trebling: the three groups of young human lovers, birds and fish. There is a treble process at work in 'Whatever is begotten, born and dies'. There is a doubling as well, in the repetition: *all* summer long, *all* neglect monuments of unageing intellect. Then comes the counterpointing of an aged man. Doubling occurs again, for emphasis, in the 'tattered coat', echoed by 'every tatter in its mortal dress'. Then comes intensification. The soul can clap its hands and sing, and louder sing, the repetition of 'sing' strengthened by 'louder'. The 'singing school' is swept on into studying; and the objects of study are the monuments formed by the sensual lovers. 'The fish, flesh, or fowl' are now counterpointed by the 'monuments of its own magnificence'.

Stanza III explains why the poem began with the word 'that' – 'That is no country for old men' – for the poet, the **persona** of the poem, has

... sailed the seas and come
To the holy city of Byzantium.

He has arrived there, he is looking back at the country (Ireland) he has left behind and is able to say dismissively 'That is no country for old men'. Years later when taking part in a BBC broadcast Yeats realised the syntax of the first line was obscure, and thought he should rewrite it as 'This [Ireland] is no country ...' In the laborious process of writing and rewriting the poem he had discarded an early version that began 'Here [in Ireland].' He also abandoned an early opening line 'This is no country for old men' and stanzas (several of them very lovely) dealing with the voyager's transition, his travelling from Ireland to Byzantium.

Stanza III again uses repetition for intensification. The sages standing in 'God's holy fire' are bidden to come from 'the holy fire'. The mosaic in the wall is 'gold', a word which will be caught up and used very effectively in the final stanza.

This third stanza is, like the first and second, concerned with singing. Stanza I's birds' song extends into the vast concept of the sensual music of youth and creativity. The soul of stanza II is to be educated by the sages who will be its singing masters. In stanza III the poet's or persona's heart is to be consumed. The 'begotten, born and dies' of the first stanza has shifted its emphasis now. The treble movement continues. The persona's heart is sick with desire (in envy of the youthful lovers) and is sick because he is aged; his heart is in fact fastened to a dying animal (the body is contrasted here with the soul). And the poet persona seeks to escape the physical end of life – death – by seeking Eternity in artifice (for art can outlast the life of its creators). The fourth, culminating stanza moves the train of thought forward rapidly, assuming eternity is beyond nature, and asserts that the poet will not take his next bodily form from any natural thing. The echo of nature in 'natural' prepares us for another emphatic repetition, 'bodily form' repeated as 'such a form'. Then the gold which we met in stanza III is repeated skilfully in the 'hammered gold and gold enamelling'.

Another contrast, between sleep and wakefulness, arrives with the drowsy emperor being kept awake by the singing of the artificial bird. It is golden, set upon a golden bough and made by goldsmiths. (Yeats's own note described how he had read 'somewhere' that there was a tree made of gold and silver in Byzantium and artificial birds that sang. Yeats was probably remembering the cover of a volume of fairy tales by Hans Andersen, on which the Emperor and his court are listening to the artificial bird. He may have been reminded of this when he was told (in about 1910) of a passage in the chronicle of Liutprand of Cremona which described the artificial singing bird in the Imperial palace.) Again the emphasis is on gold; we are, after all, in the palace, or grounds of the emperor's palace: a magnificent place. The bird is implicitly contrasted with the natural birds in the trees of the first stanza. What is it singing? We are returning to the treble action, a tripartite view of life as 'what is past, or passing, or to come'. This concept of eternity returns to the earlier phraseology of 'Whatever is begotten, born and dies', though 'dies' has now been replaced with a less finite, precise reference to what is to come after death.

The thoughts of the poem, then, are tied together in a complex pattern of contrasts, parallels, repetitions, by phrases of double and treble units. The later companion poem 'Byzantium' is even more intricate in its description of the city and the purification of the dead, carried to Paradise on the backs of dolphins. Yeats called it an example of magnificence, 'something over and above utility which wrings the heart'.

TEXT 5   AMONG SCHOOL CHILDREN

I

I walk through the long schoolroom questioning;
A kind old nun in a white hood replies;
The children learn to cipher and to sing,
To study reading-books and histories,
To cut and sew, be neat in everything
In the best modern way – the children's eyes
In momentary wonder stare upon
A sixty-year-old smiling public man.

II

I dream of a Ledaean body, bent
Above a sinking fire, a tale that she
Told of a harsh reproof, or trivial event

That changed some childish day to tragedy –
Told, and it seemed that our two natures blent
Into a sphere from youthful sympathy,
Or else, to alter Plato's parable,
Into the yolk and white of the one shell.

III
And thinking of that fit of grief or rage
I look upon one child or t'other there
And wonder if she stood so at that age –
For even daughters of the swan can share
Something of every paddler's heritage –
And had that colour upon cheek or hair,
And thereupon my heart is driven wild:
She stands before me as a living child.

IV
Her present image floats into the mind –
Did Quattrocento finger fashion it
Hollow of cheek as though it drank the wind
And took a mess of shadows for its meat?
And I though never of Ledaean kind
Has pretty plumage once – enough of that,
Better to smile on all that smile, and show
There is a comfortable kind of old scarecrow.

V
What youthful mother, a shape upon her lap
Honey of generation had betrayed,
And that must sleep, shriek, struggle to escape
As recollection or the drug decide,
Would think her son, did she but see that shape
With sixty or more winters on its head,
A compensation for the pang of his birth,
Or the uncertainty of his setting forth?

VI
Plato thought nature but a spume that plays
Upon a ghostly paradigm of things;

Solider Aristotle played the taws
Upon the bottom of a king of kings;
World-famous golden-thighed Pythagoras
Fingered upon a fiddle-stick or strings
What a star sang and careless Muses heard:
Old clothes upon old sticks to scare a bird.

VII

Both nuns and mothers worship images,
But those the candles light are not as those
That animate a mother's reveries,
But keep a marble or a bronze repose.
And yet they too break hearts – O Presences
That passion, piety or affection knows,
And that all heavenly glory symbolise –
O self-born mockers of man's enterprise;

VIII

Labour is blossoming or dancing where
The body is not bruised to pleasure soul,
Not beauty born out of its own despair,
Nor blear-eyed wisdom out of midnight oil.
O chestnut-tree, great rooted blossomer,
Are you the leaf, the blossom or the bole?
O body swayed to music, O brightening glance,
How can we know the dancer from the dance?

A prose draft of this poem written in March 1926 read: 'Topic for poem – School children and the thought that life will waste them perhaps that no possible life can fulfill our dreams or even their teacher's hope. Bring in the old thought that life prepares for what never happens'.

The poem is written in the eight-line stanzas that Yeats often used for his meditative poetry; half-rhymes are used effectively, and the skill of Yeats in using one sentence to a stanza should be observed. The poem's problems are finally solved by contemplation of the tree with its unity, what the American critic Thomas Parkinson has called 'a world of transcendent possibilities'.

Though his adherence to the usual *abababcc* rhyme scheme is not strict Yeats is using **ottava rima** for this poem which was written on 14 June 1926. The eight-line stanza obviously suits the way his thoughts and ideas progress, each stanza marking a step forward. Thus stanza I sets the scene; it ends with our seeing the poet through the eyes of the schoolchildren as 'A sixty-year-old smiling public man', public because he was a senator of the Irish Free State, established in 1922, and a winner, in 1923, of the Nobel Prize for Literature. Deeply interested in the scope and purposes of education in the new state, he was visiting a school (St Otteran's in Waterford) run on principles suggested by Maria Montessori whose *The Montessori Method* (1912) – 'the best modern way' – had suggested the need to create both spontaneity and neatness in children ('be neat in everything').

In stanza II our attention switches suddenly from the objectivity of the first (though there *is* **irony** in the description of the poet as we realise later in the poem) to a revelation of what is going on behind the smiling public mask. The poet looking at the schoolchildren is dreaming of 'a Ledaean body'. Here the cumulative effect of his poetry can come into play, for in Greek mythology Zeus, ruler of the gods and men, had taken the form of a swan to approach Leda when she was bathing in the river Eurotas, and had begotten on her the twins Castor and Pollux and a daughter, Helen. The point of this reference to Leda is at once clear to the reader who is aware of other Yeats poems in which Maud Gonne, with whom he had fallen in love in 1889 and been obsessed by throughout a great deal of his life, is compared to Helen. Helen was the beautiful wife of the King of Sparta whose running away with Paris, one of the sons of Priam, King of Troy, was the cause of the ten-year siege which ended in the Greeks sacking Troy.

The poet remembers Maud telling him of some childish troubles and this reminds him of how close their friendship was. He has obviously been reading or thinking about the Greek philosopher Plato as well as the myth of Leda and the Swan (which seemed to him 'the annunciation that founded Greece' – a union of god and human, about which he had written a poem 'Leda and the Swan' three years earlier). We don't, however, necessarily need to know Plato's *Symposium* with its story of Zeus dividing man from his original double, nearly spherical shape, into two halves, love being the attempt of humans to regain the lost unity.

Stanza III switches the poet from thoughts of Maud's childhood to the children in the school, wondering if she was like them when she was their age. Now the smiling public image conceals private truth: the poet's heart is driven wild – the last line's simplicity punching home the intensity of his emotion – at the image that comes into his mind, of her 'as a living child'. Again there comes a sudden switch in the fourth stanza which is most convincing in its presentation of the strange, unpredictable way memory and the **stream of consciousness** work, for an image of Maud as she is at present 'floats' into his mind. Her face is gaunt now – he is probably thinking of the fifteenth-century Italian artist Leonardo da Vinci (1452–1579) when he writes 'Quattrocento finger' – and though his own physical appearance was never on a level with her Ledaean beauty he thinks of his once raven black hair ('pretty plumage'), but dismisses such thoughts, and reverts to being a smiling public man. There is, however, a shock tactic in the move from the 'smiling' and 'comfortable' adjectives to the unexpected 'old scarecrow' – an image also used in 'Sailing to Byzantium', a 'tattered coat upon a stick' – which links his present appearance with hers, reminding us of their early closeness, their two natures blent together in sympathy.

Stanza V reflects upon whether a youthful mother would think her son, if she could see him at sixty, and white-haired, a compensation for the pain of childbirth and worry about the child's future. We are reminded of the poet's sixty years. ('Honey of generation' is an image taken from Porphyry's *On the Cave of the Nymphs* and refers to the pleasures of generation.)

The uncertainty of the fifth stanza leads him to think of Plato's theory of ideas or forms. These are the true objects of knowledge; they are timeless, unchanging, universal. A man who is unphilosophical is at the mercy of his sense impressions; he is like a prisoner in a cave who mistakes shadows on the wall for reality. The 'paradigm' represents an archetype, and was used by Thomas Taylor (1768–1835), a Platonist whom Yeats read, to convey the idea of essence held by Plato.

His thoughts move from Plato, interested in the individual soul, to Aristotle and his location of reality in the physical world, some of his work descriptive of the actualities of Greek life. The fact that he tutored the 'king of kings' – Alexander the Great – (the taws being a form of stick used in punishment) indicates his practicality, his potential involvement in government by shaping the youthful mind of a future great ruler; the fact of his being a more down-to-earth nature than Plato's is economically indicated by the adjective 'solider'. The third Greek philosopher who comes into Yeats's mind is Pythagoras who developed the idea of the transmigration of souls, whose golden thigh was mentioned in a life of him translated by Thomas Taylor and read by Yeats, who thought he had made measurements of the intervals between notes of music on a stretched string.

Why are these three men brought into the poem? They were teachers, and so suit a poem partially about education. But, more significantly, they were eminently famous men, and Yeats wants to show that even the greatest men also become scarecrows – 'Old clothes upon old sticks to scare a bird' – by the time they become famous. In a letter he called this stanza a fragment of his 'last curse on old age'.

The transition to stanza VII is achieved by thoughts of the nuns who teach in the school and a reversion to mothers' thoughts about their children: though the nuns worship candlelit statues, religious images, they can be affected by them, though the images are different from those of mothers. The 'Presences' are presumably both the statues and the children that are known by passion, piety or affection – another of Yeats's trebles – that symbolise heavenly glory.

The meaning of stanza VIII is difficult to analyse and describe. It can perhaps be seen within the whole structure of the poem, the first four stanzas of which deal with the difficulties of human life, the blend of youth and age, the next three which weigh up aspirations and achievements, and hint at the difference between knowledge and ignorance, something brought out in the poem's last questioning. Thus we have the question of the individual's identity at different periods of his or her life put squarely to us: Are you the leaf, the blossom or the bole? And because we are involved in the process of living – the dance – we cannot see the whole pattern of life.

Here, then, we have Yeats employing myth, and **symbolism, metrical** and intricate verbal patterns, blending them in the setting of a personal situation, expanding that with the statement of a general problem with which we all are, inevitably, involved, for it is part of the human situation, the human paradox.

Yeats sets up interactions between opposites. He balances the personal and the public. He can encompass the flux of life within the strict confines of rhyme and rhythm, within the form of a sentence which

TEXT 5 continued

usually coincides with the form of a stanza. The result is poetry of a complex texture, an intricate pattern, yet poetry which speaks directly to us. The reason is that Yeats uses the language that, as he put it, 'comes most naturally when we soliloquise'. The subtle skill, achieved over many years of labour (something naturally praised in the poem's last stanza), resulted in passionate, **rhetorical** yet normal speech, explosive because of its being tamped down into traditional form, into rhyme and metre, 'a powerful and passionate syntax'.

TEXT 6   COOLE PARK AND BALLYLEE, 1931

Under my window-ledge the waters race,
Otters below and moor-hens on the top,
Run for a mile undimmed in Heaven's face
Then darkening through 'dark' Raftery's 'cellar' drop,
Run underground, rise in a rocky place
In Coole demesne, and there to finish up
Spread to a lake and drop into a hole.
What's water but the generated soul?

Upon the border of that lake's a wood
Now all dry sticks under a wintry sun,
And in a copse of beeches there I stood,
For Nature's pulled her tragic buskin on
And all the rant's a mirror of my mood:
At sudden thunder of the mounting swan
I turned about and looked where branches break
The glittering reaches of the flooded lake.

Another emblem there! That stormy white
But seems a concentration of the sky;
And, like the soul, it sails into the sight
And in the morning's gone, no man knows why;
And is so lovely that it sets to right
What knowledge or its lack had set awry,
So arrogantly pure, a child might think
It can be murdered with a spot of ink.

Sound of a stick upon the floor, a sound
From somebody that toils from chair to chair;
Beloved books that famous hands have bound,
Old marble heads, old pictures everywhere;
Great rooms where travelled men and children found
Content or joy; a last inheritor
Where none has reigned that lacked a name and fame
Or out of folly into folly came.

A spot whereon the founders lived and died
Seemed once more dear than life; ancestral trees,
Or gardens rich in memory glorified
Marriages, alliances and families,
And every bride's ambition satisfied.
Where fashion or mere fantasy decrees
We shift about – all that great glory spent –
Like some poor Arab tribesman and his tent.

We were the last romantics – chose for theme
Traditional sanctity and loveliness;
Whatever's written in what poets name
The book of the people; whatever most can bless
The mind of man or elevate a rhyme;
But all is changed, that high horse riderless,
Though mounted in that saddle Homer rode
Where the swan drifts upon a darkening flood.

Written in Yeats's version of *ottava rima* (*ababacdd*) this poem celebrates his friend Lady Gregory while lamenting the passing of a more gracious age, a literature celebrating loveliness and sanctity. It catches the conversational tone of reminiscence, but is punctuated by questions or reflections which arise naturally out of the easy flow of the poet's thought.

He invokes the three settings with masterly skill. The lively movement of the first stanza matches the river racing past the poet's tower at Ballylee. This is set in porous limestone country where rivers can go underground in their courses. Yeats uses **alliteration** effectively, so effectively it is not so much immediately noticeable as cumulative in its effect. Thus he strengthens the repetitions of 'darkening again' in the last line of the last stanza.

Raftery's name, associated with the river's cellar (Irish: *an soilear*) drop, is introduced deliberately. Anthony Raftery (Antoine Raiftearaí, 1779–1835), a blind itinerant Irish-speaking poet, spent most of his time in south County Galway in the neighbourhood of Ballylee and Coole. Yeats wrote about him in 'The Tower II', linking him, 'beauty's blind rambling celebrant', with Homer, 'that was a blind man'. Lady Gregory had collected many of his poems and stories and details of his life – there were some people living who remembered him – and discovered his grave, paying most of the cost of a stone to mark it. She supplied Douglas Hyde with material for his 1903 edition of Raftery's poems, and translated some of his poems herself and a selection of stories. He was part of local folklore and the 'cellar' of the river named after him is still there.

The progress of the water prompts another question in the last line of the first stanza which is almost a statement, for Yeats knew that the **Neoplatonic** philosophers used water as a symbol of generation – he probably got his image from one of them, Porphyry (233–*c*.301).

The second stanza concentrates on the wintry aspect of the lake at Coole, a logical progression from the mention of it in the previous stanza. Nature seems in a tragic mood (the 'buskin' was the raised footwear used by actors in Greek tragedy) and this chimes with Yeats's feelings. He had been staying at Coole in the winter of 1931–2 to provide companionship for Lady Gregory who was suffering from cancer and died on 23 May 1932. The sudden ascent of a swan completes the picture of the lake.

The next stanza explores its meaning. The swan is an emblem, a symbol of inspiration. It is linked with the approaching death of Lady Gregory and the general mystery of life's ending for, like the soul, it is here and then 'in the morning's gone'. He rounds off the picture with an oblique reference – 'a spot of ink' – to *M. Triboulat Bonhomet* (1887), a **Symbolist** novel about a hunter of swans, by Villiers de l'Isle Adam, a French writer whose Symbolist drama *Axel* had greatly impressed Yeats in 1894.

In the fourth stanza he turns to Coole, to the house and to Lady Gregory. He had described the impressive contents of the house in his *Autobiographies*, and Lady Gregory gave an account of it in her *Coole* (1931). Part of the sadness Yeats is experiencing is that Lady Gregory is 'a last inheritor', her only son Robert, an RFC pilot, having been killed in

Italy on 23 January 1918. (Yeats wrote four poems in all in memory of him.) The previous owners – the inheritors – had been distinguished in the traditional way of many Anglo-Irish families: the 'name and fame' can be expanded by lines in Yeats's play *Purgatory*:

> Magistrates, colonels, members of Parliament,
> Captains and governors, and long ago
> Men that fought at Augrim and the Boyne.

The fifth stanza reflects upon the nature of 'Big Houses' and their demesnes. Yeats, perhaps unwittingly, suggests the tyranny such possessions exert over those who inherit them, while celebrating the long rich tradition such power-houses of memory possess. He gives us a neat vignette of the closely knit structure of county life – 'marriages, alliances and families' – and praises the permanence seemingly centred in such estates.

Yeats is, however, well aware of the socio-economic changes of his time. The days of the 'great glory' of the big houses and their encompassing estates were over. The Irish landlords' power had been declining in the nineteenth century and a series of land acts, notably the Asbourne and Wyndham Acts (of 1885 and 1903), enabling their tenants to buy the land destroyed the *raison d'être* of the greatly diminished estates which had formerly supported the big houses. And so people without continuity ('security of tenure' in modern terms) seem to the poet to resemble wandering desert Arabs.

The final stanza puts it plainly and personally. The kind of literature to which Yeats and his friends had been committed, the hopes for art they entertained, were at the mercy of change. Fashion ('or mere fantasy') had changed everything. They were the last romantics. He reverts to Raftery, whose *The Book of the People* Lady Gregory had translated, because – as he tells us in a late poem 'The Municipal Gallery Revisited' – he and his friends, especially Lady Gregory and Synge, thought that contact with the soil should be the basis of their writing, itself the 'Dream of the noble and the beggar-man'.

This poem reminds us of the poignant, compressed, comfortless questioning of 'Nineteen Hundred and Nineteen':

> Man is in love and loves what vanishes,
> What more is there to say?

So no-one now mounts Pegasus, the winged horse of Greek mythology, the favourite of the Muses, though Homer had done so (Pegasus, a lively colt, had seemed earlier to have been reduced to carthorse duties in 'The Fascination of What's Difficult', a poem of 1909/1910, which complained that the business of directing the Abbey Theatre had kept Yeats from writing poetry). With Homer as a reminder of the greatness of the traditional sanctity and loveliness that now appeared diminished, already becoming part of a very different past, the poem ends upon a sombre elegaic and dark note, returning us – in a subtle way – to enriched images, first to the darkening water of the first stanza, then to a linkage of blind Homer and dark Raftery, as the swan now drifts upon a darkening flood. The complexity of the poem's texture, its movement from river to lake to house, to Lady Gregory, to the established aristocratic families, to great art, and then to the lake again is Yeats at his best, blending personal with public issues, and doing it with a controlled intensity of emotion and thought.

PART FIVE

BACKGROUND

YEATS'S LIFE AND WORK

William Butler Yeats was born on 13 June 1865 at 'George's Ville', No. 1 Sandymount Avenue, Dublin. His father, John Butler Yeats, had been expected to follow the careers of his father and his grandfather and become a Church of Ireland clergyman, but he opted for the law and trained as a barrister before deciding to become an artist. The poet's mother, born Susan Pollexfen, was a member of a well-to-do family in Sligo, in the west of Ireland, which owned ships and a milling company. At the time of his son's birth John Butler Yeats was living on rents from over 300 acres of inherited land in County Kildare. As a landlord, about to become a barrister, he had seemed a most acceptable son-in-law to the Pollexfens. But when he moved to London in 1867 to study painting and the income of the heavily mortgaged lands diminished, Susan and the children (after W.B. came two daughters and the youngest son, Jack, who later became a very famous artist; another son, Robert, died in 1873) spent much time with her parents in Sligo because John Butler Yeats was impractical where money was concerned. He failed to charge enough for his portraits and often went on painting and repainting them for too long. Thus Yeats grew up in an atmosphere of genteel poverty; like so many Irish writers, he had well-to-do, better-off relatives, but in his own family money was always very short.

By 1880 the income from the family lands in Kildare finally ceased, and the family moved back to Ireland. From 1875 to 1880 Willie Yeats had been at the Godolphin School in Hammersmith; from 1880 to 1883 he went to the High School, Dublin, learning much about poetry from his father when both of them took the train from Howth – the peninsula forming the northern arm of Dublin Bay – to the city, to breakfast together at the artist's studio near the boy's school. Then came the question of a career – Willie was unlikely to pass the easy entrance examination to Trinity College Dublin, so he entered the School of Art in Dublin; then he decided that he wanted to be a poet and his father encouraged him in this, making light of the need to earn a living. 'A gentleman is not concerned with getting-on' he would say, somewhat fecklessly, making the best of the poverty to which he had condemned his family. Instead of financial security, he gave his children the stimulus of ideas in endlessly challenging conversations, and he encouraged them to develop their own talents.

In Dublin Willie Yeats met John O'Leary, a former Fenian, who interested him in nationalism and translations of Irish writing into English; by doing so he gave him fresh and exciting subject matter for his poetry and a new purpose. Now not only would he write about the places, the stories, the supernatural beliefs he met in Sligo, but he would give the old Irish legends new expression in English, recreating, he thought, Ireland's largely forgotten intellectual heritage. He was stimulated by reading Sir Samuel Ferguson's translations, as well as James Clarence Mangan's versions of Irish poems, and, particularly, Standish O'Grady's histories and fiction. His own treatment of material from Irish legend bloomed in *The Wanderings of Oisin* in 1889.

This was the year he met Maud Gonne, tall and beautiful, a well-to-do revolutionary with whom he fell in love. Penniless, he could only offer her poetic devotion: he wrote a play, *The Countess Kathleen*, for her, and many love poems, wistful and melancholic. In 1891 he proposed to her but was refused in the words Maud Gonne used subsequently on many similar occasions; the world would thank her for not marrying him, she said, they should continue to be friends, and he should go on writing lovely poetry for her.

He joined the Theosophists (who believed that knowledge of God could be attained through spiritual ecstasy and direct intuition), only to be asked to leave because of his desire for evidence. Yeats also became interested in what was then considered unorthodox thought: Buddhism, magic, spiritualism, astrology, the Cabbala. He joined the Order of the Golden Dawn, a Rosicrucian order, in 1890. He edited Blake, he read Swedenborg and Boehme. This side of his life he kept apart from his poetry at first; his prose consisted of articles on and reviews of Irish literature, and collections of Irish fairy and folk tales. In 1891 he thought the time ripe, after the death of Parnell (the leader of the Irish Parliamentary party whose involvement in a divorce case had split the party) had brought a lull to Irish politics, for launching a literary movement. He formed Irish literary societies in Dublin and London. He told Maud Gonne what he was doing for Ireland was as important as the political work of more obvious nationalists, though for a time he and she were members of the Irish Republican Brotherhood, a secret revolutionary organisation.

During the 1890s Yeats's poetry became more obscure. He moved from his early echoes of Indian and pastoral poetry, from relatively simple poems about Irish places and fairy legends, to poetry using the material of the Irish cycles of tales, the stories of Ulster and the Fenian tales, developing readers' awareness of the heroes and heroines of these legends – Fergus, Conchubar, Cuchulain and Naoise; Maeve, Emer and Deirdre. His book of poems and stories *The Celtic Twilight* (1893) gave its name to the kind of literature produced by Yeats himself and his imitators: romantic, affirmative, sometimes vague, misty, dreamy and wistful. Yeats was using his 'Celtic' material in a more and more complex visionary way; he had to explain the meanings of his poems in increasingly lengthy notes, glossing his Irish material, explaining, for instance, such names as Tuatha da Danaan, Sidhe or Aengus, discussing the **symbolism** of the Rose, and relating the contents of poems to the beliefs of country people and those beliefs in turn to other traditions such as vegetation myths or fertility rites. *The Wind Among the Reeds* (1899) is the culmination of this 'Celtic' poetry, mysterious, vague and beautiful.

Yeats's life changed towards the end of the century. He met Lady Gregory in London in 1894, first visited her in Ireland in 1896, and from 1897 tended to spend his summers at Coole Park, her house in County Galway. She lent him money so that he was able to give up the journalism which had brought him a minute income (never over £150 a year before 1900) and concentrate on his own writing. He repaid her loans later out of the proceeds of lecturing in America. At the age of thirty he had left the family home in Bedford Park, London, in 1896, sharing rooms for a time with his friend Arthur Symons in the Temple, then renting his own set of rooms in Woburn Buildings in London. The reason for his taking these rooms was his brief affair – his first experience of sex – with Olivia Shakespear, unhappily married to a solicitor fourteen years her senior, a highly intelligent woman, very well read and also a talented novelist. The long summers he spent at Coole gave him a peaceful, ordered existence, and Lady Gregory invited other writers to the house, among them Yeats's friend George Russell (1867–1935) whose pen-name was AE, George

Bernard Shaw (1856–1950), George Moore (1853–1933) and many other Irish authors and artists. She also rekindled his interest in folk tales and speech, and he encouraged her in her excellent translations of the Irish tales, the best known being *Cuchulain of Muirthemne* (1902) and *Gods and Fighting Men* (1904).

Yeats's unrequited love for Maud Gonne had made him increasingly unhappy during the 1890s; he had become disillusioned with the Irish nationalists and with the revolutionaries (particularly after seeing the effects of rioting in Dublin in 1897). In 1903 Maud Gonne's marriage to John MacBride put an end to his hopes that one day she would marry him. The love poetry he continued to write still recorded his love for her, but it had become a love which had no future. The 'old high way of love' was replaced by realism, by knowledge of how she had never really understood his aims, of how he had grown out of fashion 'like an old song'. And yet the poems continue to celebrate her beauty, her stature and the fineness of spirit he had discerned in her. His poetry had begun to develop a new style, stripped of decoration, where nouns and verbs became more telling than adjectives, where the poet might 'wither into truth'.

Yeats found work which was to employ his energies: 'theatre business, management of men'. With Lady Gregory's considerable aid he brought an Irish Theatre into being. They were helped by George Moore and Edward Martyn at first, then by John Millington Synge (1871–1909). Irish plays, first staged in halls, found a permanent home in the Abbey Theatre in Dublin, converted out of a former morgue, and financed in its initial years by an Englishwoman, Annie Horniman. Yeats was manager of the Abbey from its inception in 1904 until 1910. This was not easy work, and it was not aided by those who objected on religious grounds to Yeats's *The Countess Kathleen* and on puritanical-nationalist grounds to Synge's plays which did not, they thought, portray Ireland as she should be portrayed. This led, in the case of Synge's *The Playboy of the Western World*, to riots in 1907 which disillusioned Yeats deeply, though he insisted on staging Synge's play; it seemed to him that many of the public disliked the art he and his friends were working so hard to write and produce.

After this Lady Gregory, her son Robert and Yeats went to Italy; it was his first visit and a revelation of what enlightened aristocratic patronage had done for the arts in Italy. Here was a vital contrast: between the mob howling down great art in Ireland, and what had been created by aristocratic patrons in Urbino and Florence, in Sienna and Ravenna. But Yeats was to experience still more disillusion with Ireland, for when Lady Gregory's nephew, Sir Hugh Lane (1875–1915) offered his superb collection of French paintings to Dublin, the Corporation cavilled at the gift which Lane had made conditional upon his pictures being properly housed. (He himself favoured a design for a gallery over the River Liffey.) Yeats hurled himself into the controversy that arose, and began to write angry political poems contrasting Irish patrons with past Italian ducal munificence and vision. He contrasted, too, Irish nationalists with those of the past, to the denigration of contemporary leaders.

'All changed, changed utterly', wrote Yeats in 'Easter 1916', deeply moved by the unexpected rising in Ireland which, as he realised, made martyrs of the leaders executed for their part in it. He had been in France when it occurred, staying with Maud Gonne in her house in Normandy. Her marriage had lasted but two years; she obtained a separation from MacBride and retired from public life. She had a child, Sean, by MacBride, and had had two children earlier by Lucien Millevoye (a French journalist and follower of General Boulanger), a boy who died in 1891 and a girl, Iseult, born in 1894 (Yeats was unaware of this liaison until 1898). MacBride was one of the leaders executed in Dublin in 1916, and Yeats proposed marriage to Maud again, to be refused in her customary way. Later he proposed to Iseult who enjoyed flirting with him and would not give him an answer. He returned to France in 1917 to propose again. This time he issued an ultimatum to Iseult; when she came to London she must say yea or nay – if the latter he would marry a girl whom he had known for some years. Iseult refused him, and he married Georgie Hyde Lees on 20 October 1917. She was twenty-six, he fifty-two, and the marriage transformed his life.

Shortly after their marriage Mrs Yeats (now called George not Georgie) took up automatic writing, and Yeats was greatly excited by this, as it seemed to offer him a system of thought. He wrote to his father that 'the setting of it all in order' had helped him with his verse, 'has given me a new framework and new patterns'. *A Vision* (1925) incorporated in its system his ideas on history and human personality. His *Collected Works* had appeared in an eight-volume edition in 1908, and it might have seemed then that his poetic career was over, but now that he was working on *A Vision* his poetry took on vigorous new life. The disillusionment which had marked the poems of *The Green Helmet* (1910) and *Responsibilities* (1914) and some of the poems of *The Wild Swans at Coole* (1919) gave way to a new creativity, in which Yeats incorporated the beauty of his early poetry along with the bare strength he had learned to express in his middle period, achieving the rich texture of his mature manner.

He found new confidence in his marriage, which had assured the continuance of the Yeats line, for two children, Anne and Michael, were born in 1919 and 1921 respectively. His marriage was romantically based on the first house Yeats owned, his tower in the west of Ireland, and practically on the subsequent purchase of a fine house in Merrion Square, Dublin; his new confidence was grounded in what Yeats praised in 'Under Saturn' as the wisdom his wife had brought to their marriage, the comfort she had made. There was, in addition, the international public recognition given to his poetry by the award of the Nobel Prize for literature, in 1923, and that given to his standing as an Irish public man by his appointment as a senator of the newly created Irish Free State. The poetry of *Michael Robartes and the Dancer* (1921) included not only 'Easter 1916' but 'The Second Coming' with its bleak anticipation of coming ruin and chaos, and 'A Prayer for my Daughter', with its hope that his daughter might avoid the errors of such opinionated beauties as Maud Gonne and follow instead the courtesy and glad kindness he appreciated in his young wife.

The Tower (1928) contained a magnificent range of poems; personal in such things as the particular meanings he attached to the city of Byzantium in 'Sailing to Byzantium', the local history and legend attaching to his tower in County Galway and its neighbourhood, but universal in their treatment of the human problems of age; the descent of inherited characteristics in families; the bitterness of civil war; and the whole question, in 'Among School Children', of the meaning of life itself. There were poems which continued the matter of *A Vision*, such as 'Two Songs from a Play' or 'Leda and the Swan' as well as poems of past love, and poems in the series *A Man Young and Old* expressing love as if a man young and old were speaking them, balanced by the later series *A Woman Young and Old* in *The Winding Stair and other Poems* (1933).

This volume reflects Yeats's interest in the Irish writers of the eighteenth century, whom he had come to read after his marriage. His Irish reading in his twenties and thirties had been of translations of Irish literature or of authors known more in Ireland than outside it – Irish novelists, for instance, such as Carleton, the Banim brothers, Kickham and Emily Lawless. In his middle period he had been rereading Shakespeare and rereading and editing Spenser, as well as studying Chaucer and discovering Landor and Donne. But he found his true intellectual ancestry in Swift (whom he had earlier not regarded as Irish), Berkeley, Goldsmith and Burke. He paid tribute to them not only in poems such as 'The Seven Sages', but in his prose, notably in the Introduction to *The Words upon the Window-Pane* – included in *Wheels and Butterflies* (1934) – his superbly realistic, atmospheric play about a seance and the ghostly presence of Swift. His *Four Plays for Dancers* (1921) had been designed, under the influence of Japanese Noh drama, for small select audiences, but later some of his plays were again written for and produced in the Abbey.

In the 1920s and 1930s Yeats's health caused anxiety: high blood pressure in 1924, a bleeding lung in 1927, Malta fever in 1929, the Steinach operation in 1934, heart missing a beat and nephritis in 1936. None of this diminished his output, though it meant the abandonment of the tower (damp and not very comfortable) as a summer residence after 1929, and subsequent winter visits south in search of sunshine to France, Italy and Spain. Lady Gregory died in 1932 and the Yeats family then gave up the Dublin town house in Merrion Square, leasing for thirteen years a small old farmhouse with attractive grounds at Rathfarnham at the foot of the Dublin mountains. Yeats had made new friends in England and visited Lady Gerald Wellesley in Cornwall in 1937 and 1938 and the Heald sisters in Sussex in 1938. His last public appearance was in the Abbey Theatre in August 1938; he died at Roquebrune in France on 28 January 1939, still writing poetry within days of his death.

OTHER WORKS BY YEATS

The youthful poet found he could earn money by journalism, by writing on Irish topics for Irish and American journals, then reaching wider literary audiences by contributions to such journals as the *Scots Observer*, the *Nation*, the *National Observer*, the *Bookman*, the *Speaker* and the *Academy*. His first prose anthology *Fairy and Folk Tales of the Irish Peasantry* (1888) drew on already published work and he followed it with *Irish Fairy Tales* (1892). He began to find the peasantry more interesting than fairies and so selected material from Irish fiction which dealt with them, first with his *Stories from Carleton* (1899) – William Carleton (1794–1869), a bilingual novelist, had conveyed the nature of rural Catholic Ireland very effectively – and then with his excellent two-volume *Representative Irish Tales* (1891). Next he tried his hand at fiction, writing *John Sherman and Dhoya* (1891) under the pseudonym Gangonagh, the former a short realistic novel, the latter a mythological story.

Of his early prose *The Celtic Twilight* (1893) became widely known; it contained previously published essays on Irish subjects as well as material from *Fairy and Folk Tales of the Irish Peasantry*. Originally Yeats's prose style had been simple, but in the 1890s, under the influence of the **Symbolists**, of Oscar Wilde and Walter Pater, it became decorative, allusive and mannered. His stories of *The Secret Rose* (1897) were written in an artificial, elaborate English, as were such essays as 'The Autumn of the Body' (1898) and 'The Symbolism of Poetry'. In 1896 he began work on a novel *The Speckled Bird* but never completed it – the several versions have been published posthumously. By 1900 he had begun to write more directly, as in his essay 'The Philosophy of Shelley's Poetry'.

Yeats's most original criticism is probably to be found in his views on drama, shaped during the creation and early years of the Irish national theatre: for ten years he expressed his ideals and defended them in occasional publications, *Beltaine*, *Samhain* and *The Arrow*.

His interest in magic and the occult emerged in *Per Amica Silentia Lunae* (1918), essays dealing with the idea of the mask, the self and anti-self, and the daimon. He gave these ideas expanded, altered utterance in *A Vision* (1926), which added to his earlier reading in heterodox material his new studies of history and philosophy and owed a great deal to his wife's automatic writing. He became deeply interested in eighteenth-century Irish writing and this interest was reflected in various essays.

The first of Yeats's autobiographical writings appeared in *Reveries over Childhood and Youth* (1916). His selection of events, his defining them, shaping and interpreting them, his use of the background, all create a pattern. His capacity to mythologise irradiates his prose with memorable phrases and gives rich insights into particular moments in his life. He had learned a lot from his studies in Symbolism, his search for essences. His capacity for appreciation and admiration emerged in *The Bounty of Sweden* (1925) celebrating his visit to Stockholm to receive the Nobel Prize for literature while his sardonic humour was unleashed in *Dramatis Personae* (1935).

His *Essays* (1924) continued his idiosyncratic critical reactions to literature. Ten years later *Wheels and Butterflies* demonstrated further developments of his ideas, while *On the Boiler* (1939) indulged his capacity to shock as well as explore his own ideas frankly and freely. He wrote many prefaces and introductions to the work of other authors (they have been collected in *Prefaces and Introductions*, ed. William H. O'Donnell (1988).) Among them is a model for all bureaucrats in the simple, direct prose of 'What we did or tried to do', in *Coinage of Saorstat Eiream* (1928), his report as chairman of the Senate Committee which gave Ireland a beautiful coinage.

An admirably evocative prose writer (who could produce such sentences as: 'The poet finds and makes his mask in disappointment, the hero in defeat', or 'We make out of the quarrel with others **rhetoric**, but of the quarrel with ourselves, poetry'), Yeats is also to be considered as a playwright. He wrote plays all his life from the verse plays of his teens and early twenties. Seeing his *The Land of Heart's Desire* performed in 1894, and later *The Countess Kathleen*, intensified his desire for an Irish theatre, and the explosive success of his *Cathleen ni Houlihan* in 1902 gave him much credit in nationalist circles. Other plays followed: *The King's Threshold*, *Where There is Nothing*, *The Shadowy Waters* and his own anticipation of the techniques of Japanese Noh drama (to which Ezra Pound later introduced him), *On Baile's Strand* in which he gave the Cuchulain legend dramatic treatment – a theme that he used frequently in his work. *The Green Helmet* is an engaging play, and the strange exotic quality of *The Player Queen* (1922) emerges extremely effectively on stage.

Yeats tired of writing for the Abbey Theatre for a time and decided instead to write plays for small audiences, the result the *Four Plays for Dancers* which are concentrated in the manner of the Noh. *The Words Upon the Window-Pane* (1934), however, was a return to drama for the public stage, and *The Herne's Egg* (1938) and *Purgatory* (1938) were also produced in the Abbey, the latter a compelling piece of compression.

The extent of Yeats's prose is indeed impressive. *The Collected Letters*, emerging volume by volume at present, show the energy and honesty he put into his correspondence. Among the day-to-day recording of events – the minutiae, say, of the theatre business of the Abbey – there are gems of apprehension, sharp *aperçus* and anecdotes, and a blending of personal attitudes to people and literature, to public events and private reflections. The letters show us a man of original mind communicating openly and most effectively to his friends.

HISTORICAL BACKGROUND

Eighteen-ninety-one is a crucial date in Yeats's career. That year Parnell died. He had been a powerful political leader who through the Land League had won the war for the land – the landlords were bought out by the tenants in a series of acts: he had been on the brink of achieving Home Rule (the Act of Union of 1800 had abolished the parliament in Dublin replacing it with Irish MPs in Westminster) through his brilliant tactics in the House of Commons where the Irish party under his leadership held the balance of power. But Parnell loved Kitty O'Shea, a married woman, and was cited in a divorce case by her husband. Parnell refused to resign his leadership, despite Gladstone, the Liberal prime minister, turning against him, the Catholic church in Ireland attacking him and a majority of the Irish party voting for his resignation. Yeats realised the time was opportune, in the stagnation of Irish politics after Parnell's death, to launch the Literary Movement.

Various organisations, the Gaelic Athletic Association (founded 1884) and the Gaelic League (founded 1893), were promoting the revival of national feeling in sport and in the attempt to keep the Irish language alive (it had declined since the famine). Yeats's founding literary societies in Dublin and London and establishing the Irish National Theatre in the

Abbey Theatre in Dublin stemmed from his nationalist views. He had moved from supporting Home Rule to wanting to create an Ireland which would be intellectually and spiritually true to its past culture and be independent of English attitudes. In this he was continuing the long tradition of anticolonialism begun by Swift – though he did not realise the political nature of Swift's writing until much later.

Yeats joined the IRB (the Irish Republican Brotherhood), which replaced the Fenian Brotherhood (financed by people of Irish descent in the United States who, embittered by the famine and the need for their ancestors to emigrate, wanted to overthrow British rule in Ireland); the IRB later became the IRA. Yeats, disillusioned by his experiences in chairing the association set up to celebrate the centenary of the 1798 Revolution, and by the potential violence of the revolutionary nationalists, left the organisation about 1900. The Irish party succeeded in getting a Home Rule bill passed in 1914 but it was shelved for the duration of the war in which many Irishmen fought in the British forces. An Ulster Volunteer force was set up in the largely Presbyterian north-east of Ireland to resist Home Rule and in reaction to it an Irish Volunteer force was established in the rest of Ireland and the nationalist areas of the north. Other forces developed; Sinn Fein was founded by Arthur Griffiths in 1901; the Irish Citizen Army was led by James Larkin. A small group, inside the Irish Volunteers (some were members of the IRB) decided on the Easter rising in 1916 although knowing it had no chance of success. It had little support in Ireland until the execution of sixteen of its leaders renewed nationalistic enthusiasm. Sinn Fein held seventy-three seats in the election of 1918, but instead of going to Westminster met in an illegal assembly or parliament in Dublin called Dail Eireann. A war for independence began in 1919 between the IRA and the British forces, which were augmented by the Black and Tans, a paramilitary force. A truce was declared in 1921 and the Anglo-Irish Treaty signed in 1922, dividing Ireland into a twenty-six-county Irish Free State and the six-county Ulster, which had been given its own parliament in 1920. A civil war broke out in June 1922 between the Republicans who opposed the treaty (because it abandoned the ideal of an all-Ireland republic and involved an oath of allegiance to the British crown) and those who supported it. The bitter civil war lasted a year and was marked by many acts of violence and cruelty.

Yeats, who became a senator in the Upper House of the Irish Free State in 1923, had an armed guard and, apart from his 'Meditations in Time of Civil War', recorded in a letter an incident in the civil war when the bridge leading to his tower was blown up. He contributed to Senate debates and described its activities as like those of coral insects. De Valera, who had led the Republicans, created a new party, Fianna Fail, in 1926; its members eventually took their seats in the Dail and formed a government in 1932. A new constitution was introduced in 1937 which claimed power over the thirty-two counties of Ireland, though in effect it is the constitution of the twenty-six counties; Fianna Fail remained in power from 1932 to 1948 and de Valera adopted a policy of neutrality in the Second World War.

LITERARY BACKGROUND

Victorian literature inherited Romanticism and continued it. Enhanced awareness became a compensation for the daily 'realities' of an increasingly complex life while ideas were still largely based upon feeling. Yeats later described himself as a last Romantic. Work by the poetic giants of the Victorian age was still being published when his first impressive poem *The Wanderings of Oisin* appeared in 1889. Browning died that year but the poet laureate, Tennyson, lived on to 1892. Dante Gabriel Rossetti, the Pre-Raphaelite who so influenced Yeats, had died in 1882, but his associates, William Morris, whose use of legend appealed greatly to Yeats, and who had learned hatred of modern civilisation from Ruskin (another of Yeats's mentors), and Swinburne, whose virtuosity Yeats admired, were both writing vigorously, as were Meredith and Patmore.

Yeats, working hard to establish himself in the literary world of London, thought that poets should know one another in case they became jealous of one another's success. He became one of the founders of the Rhymers' Club in 1891 which included Lionel Johnson, Ernest Dowson, John Davidson and Arthur Symons. He later saw his fellow poets as turning from money-making; they were poor and many of them were unhappy in their exploration of new subjects. Drugs, harlots, music halls obsessed some of them in their search for heightened awareness.

Yeats was impressed by the poise of Oscar Wilde and Lionel Johnson. From Symons he learned about the French **Symbolists**. The Decadent poets of the 1890s, the avant-garde *Yellow Book* with its drawings by Aubrey Beardsley and their challenge to Victorian respectability, however, were only one aspect of the period. W.E. Henley (1849–1903) was an editor under whom Yeats said he, like many others, began his education. The others included R.L. Stevenson, Shaw, Rudyard Kipling and Thomas Hardy. Henley saw himself as countering the aesthetic movement (which he called the new effeminacy) and the Decadent spirit represented by Wilde; the conservative magazines he edited were patriotic, supportive of the Empire, and 'virile'. Victorian authors continued to write into the twentieth century. Hardy, for instance, left off novel-writing with *Jude the Obscure* (1895) and turned to poetry. Though his 'epic spectacle', *The Dynasts* (3 parts, 1904; 1906; 1908) was nineteenth century in concept, Hardy had a telling influence on English poetry in the twentieth century. He was traditional in his respect for form, concentrating with astringency upon details, upon scenes charged with emotional recreation of events. Robert Bridges, too, linked nineteenth and twentieth centuries, his shorter poems justifying his becoming poet laureate in 1913, but his longer poem *Testament of Beauty* (1929) is so self-consciously literary that it is not often read. Max Beerbohm, a *Yellow Book* author, echoed the Wildean strain, and continued to parody his contemporaries effectively well into the twentieth century.

Georgian Poetry 1911–12, the first of five anthologies, contained such poets as Lascelles Abercrombie, Rupert Brooke, G.K. Chesterton, W.H. Davies, Walter de la Mare, James Elroy Flecker, John Masefield and Harold Munro. The **Georgians** took up homely subjects, tried to write directly about them and set out over-deliberately to make beauty, often creating banality instead.

The poets of the First World War included Brooke whose war **sonnets** were full of early exultation at the war. Its grimmer realities were conveyed by Charles Sorley, Isaac Rosenberg, Ivor Gurney, Siegfried Sassoon, Wilfred Owen and Edmund Blunden. Edward Thomas, who died in the trenches in 1917, created a new kind of poetry, authentic, spare, and forthright. Robert Graves was scarred by the war, but wrote poems of **metaphysical** self-revelation, honest and technically assured.

David Jones – in the same regiment as Sassoon and Graves – did not make use of his wartime experience until *In Parenthesis* (1937).

Modernism belongs to the second and third decades of the twentieth century. While older authors such as Hardy, Joseph Conrad, Shaw, Arnold Bennett and George Moore continued to write, and were accompanied by the newer writers such as John Masefield, Sassoon, Aldous Huxley and Lytton Strachey, literary experimentation was in full swing. In novel writing D.H. Lawrence's *Sons and Lovers* (1913) and *Women in Love* (1916), Joyce's *A Portrait of the Artist as a Young Man* (1916) and *Ulysses* (1922), Ford Madox Ford's *The Good Soldier* (1915) and *Some do Not* (1924), Virginia Woolf's *Mrs Dalloway* (1925) and *To the Lighthouse* (1927) marked a period of intense artistic innovation. In poetry T.S. Eliot's *Prufrock* (1917) and *The Waste Land* (1922), Edith Sitwell's *Façade* (1922) and Yeats's *The Wild Swans at Coole* (1919) and *Michael Robartes and the Dancer* (1922) show strikingly new and differing sensibilities.

In Yeats's case – and in Eliot's – much was owed to Ezra Pound, who came from America to England and first joined forces with the **Imagists**, Richard Aldington and Hilda Doolittle. With his doctrine of 'make it new' he encouraged Yeats, who had already begun to change his style, to strengthen it, with symbolism no longer used as decoration, to reach new diversities of tone, to attempt new illumination of subject matter with searching self-honesty. Another to influence Yeats was his Irish friend and one-time fellow senator, Oliver St John Gogarty, a gifted minor poet, a surgeon, novelist and autobiographer; his capacity for witty bawdry probably spawned the Crazy Jane poems. There are many echoes in subject matter as well as style in their work of the 1920s and 1930s. Yeats's awareness of the poets of the 1930s – W.H. Auden, Louis MacNeice, Stephen Spender and Cecil Day Lewis – came when he selected poems for the *Oxford Book of Modern Verse* (1926), a highly idiosyncratic anthology.

PART SIX

CRITICAL HISTORY & FURTHER READING

EARLY RECEPTION

To examine chronologically the critical reception Yeats's changing and developing poetry has received is to realise how greatly criticism itself has changed since Yeats began writing. Early criticism of his work was mainly descriptive. The discussion of his 'Celtic' material was superficial, for few critics (with the exception of his friends, John Todhunter, Lionel Johnson, Arthur Symons and George Russell, and William Sharp who also wrote as Fiona Macleod) knew much about the source material he was using; and even fewer recognised the magic and mysticism he increasingly introduced into his poetry of the 1890s.

Many reviewers complained that he did not write enough, but the appearance of the eight volumes of his *Collected Works* in 1908 should have made critical assessment easier. Few critics, however, realised immediately the significance of the change in his poetry at the turn of the century from escapism to greater realism. Ezra Pound's review of *Responsibilities* (1914) welcomed the new stronger style. To describe Yeats's poetry as 'Celtic' and 'mystical' was no longer enough. Pound regarded him as the greatest living poet writing in English, and his review was a landmark.

The first book-length study, by the Ulster novelist Forrest Reid, published in 1915, dwelt more on the early achievement, but by 1921 the Irish poet and playwright Padraic Colum, reviewing Yeats's *Selected Poems* (1921) was discerning in his praise of the great austere thrilling lyrics written between 1904 and 1914. At first not many critics recognised the subsequent flowering of Yeats's new manner (with elements of the early apprehension of beauty blended with the tough awareness of middle age) after his marriage in 1917. The *Times Literary Supplement*'s reviewer saw the new poetry as racy and passionate, appreciating the 'new surprise of meaning' got out of the old tunes that Yeats could play in such a masterly way. The full impact of Yeats's mature poetry did not fully register until the publication of *The Tower* (1928).

The Irish poet and critic Austin Clarke found in this volume, despite the personal disquiet, an imaginative and prosodic beauty conveying 'the pure and impersonal joy of art'. Two American critics, John Gould Fletcher and Theodore Spencer, also hailed the achievement of *The Tower* but it was another American, Edmund Wilson, who proved able, in *Axel's Castle* (1931), to appreciate just what Yeats was doing.

Mid twentieth-century criticism

It was not until after Yeats died in 1939 that criticism and scholarship burgeoned. Joseph Hone's biography of 1942 led the way. The fact that in that year the large winter number of the *Southern Review* was devoted to Yeats demonstrated a rapidly growing critical interest in his work, something encouraged by the publication of the expanded *Collected Poems* (1950) and the *Collected Plays* (1952) which meant Yeats's later work – previously published in small editions – became more readily available. Variorum editions of the *Poems* (1957) and the *Plays* (1968) indicated the extent of Yeats's revisions of his texts; the extent of his writing was shown by Wade's *Bibliography* (1951; 3rd edn 1968: a new, much larger Bibliography is being edited by Colin Smythe). Wade also edited a one-volume collection of Yeats's *Letters* (1954) and Macmillan produced a uniform edition of his prose. Now two impressive scholarly projects are in progress, volume by volume, the *Collected Edition of the Works of W.B. Yeats* and the *Collected Letters*. All these provide us with fresh information as well as excellent texts.

In the 1940s scholars and critics began to explore the relationship between Yeats's life and work which is still continuing. Among them were Denis Donoghue, Richard Ellmann, T.R. Henn, A. Norman Jeffares, Augustine Martin, A.G. Stock and Peter Ure, whose works can be found in most libraries. They are largely appreciative. Adverse criticism, some of it verging on the ridiculous, has been written by F.R. Leavis, Robert Graves, D.S. Savage and Ivor Winters.

Specialised studies

Others deal with particular aspects of his work in highly specialised studies: only a few of these can be mentioned here for reasons of space.

They include Hazard Adams (Yeats and Blake); Brian Atkins (Greek and Roman themes); Elizabeth Cullingford (Yeats and politics; something also dealt with by Conor Cruise O'Brien, whose views were refuted by Patrick Cosgrave); George Mills Harper (the occult, and an edition of the scripts of Mrs Yeats's automatic writing); Ellic Howe (The Golden Dawn); Giorgio Melchiori (the visual arts, also dealt with by Elizabeth B. Loizeaux (Yeats and art)); Virginia Moore (occult symbolism and esoteric knowledge, also treated by F.A.C. Wilson); Thomas Parkinson and Jon Stallworthy (the later poems); Donald T. Torchiana (Yeats and Georgian Ireland); Helen Hennessy Vendler (*A Vision*, also discussed by Thomas Whitaker and edited by A. Norman Jeffares) and Brenda Webster (a misguided attempt to interpret Yeats in Freudian terms). *Yeats and Women*, ed. Deirdre Toomey (1997) is an invaluable guide to the subject.

COMMENTARIES AND BIOGRAPHIES

Various detailed explanations of and commentaries on the poems have been written, among them those of A. Norman Jeffares, Edward Malins, George Brandon Saul and John Unterecker; and several collections of critical essays have been published. There has been much biographical interest. Frank Tuohy, *Yeats* (1976); Augustine Martin, *W.B. Yeats: an introductory life* (1983; rev. edn 1990); A. Norman Jeffares, *Yeats: a New Biography* (1988); A.D.F. Macrae, *Yeats: a Literary Life* (1995); Keith Alldrit, *W.B. Yeats: The Man and the Milieu* (1997); R.F. Foster, *A Life*, Vol. I, *The Apprentice Mage* (1865–1914) (1997); Stephen Coote, *W.B. Yeats: a life* (1997); and Brenda Maddox, *George's Ghosts: A New Life of W.B. Yeats* (1999). Finally, William M. Murphy's *Prodigal Father: the Life of John Butler Yeats 1839–1922* (1978) supplies much information about W.B. Yeats.

FURTHER READING

YEATS'S POETRY

W.B. Yeats, *Collected Poems* (1950)

– *The Poems. A New Edition*, ed. Richard Finneran (1984)

Based on the *Collected Poems* (1950) but containing additional poems, sixty-two taken from the *Variorum Edition*, others being lyrics taken from within larger works. The editor has used a multitude of sources for poems from *The Winding Stair and Other Poems* to the end of Yeats's life

– *Yeats's Poems*, ed. A. Norman Jeffares (3rd edition, 1996)
Based on the chronological order and text of *The Poems of W.B. Yeats*, (2 vols, 1949). An appendix by Warwick Gould discusses the order of the poems

– *Collected Poems*, ed. Augustine Martin (1990)
Based largely on *Collected Poems* (1950) with some idiosyncratic alterations in the order of the poems and two additions

– *W.B. Yeats: The Poems*, ed. Daniel Albright (1990)
Draws eclectically upon various versions of the texts at the editor's whim, utilising much information from A. Norman Jeffares, *A New Commentary on Yeats's Poems* (1968; 1984)

–*The Variorum Edition of the Poems of W.B. Yeats*, ed. Peter Allt and Russell K. Alspach (1957)
All editors owe a great deal to this edition which is based upon *The Poems of W.B. Yeats* (2 vols, 1949). This gives full details of the many changes Yeats made to the texts of his poems in the course of successive printings or editions

A SELECT BIBLIOGRAPHY OF OTHER WORKS BY YEATS

SELECTIONS

W.B. Yeats, *Selected Plays*, ed. A. Norman Jeffares, Macmillan (revised and expanded edn) 1991

W.B. Yeats, *Selected Criticism and Prose*, ed. A. Norman Jeffares, Pan Books, 1980

COMPLETE TEXTS
W.B. Yeats, *Collected Plays*, Macmillan, 1934 and subsequent printings

– *Autobiographies*, Macmillan, 1956

– *Mythologies*, Macmillan, 1959

–*Essays and Introductions*, Macmillan, 1962

– *Explorations*, Macmillan, 1962

– *Memoirs*, ed. Denis Donoghue, Macmillan 1972

– *Uncollected Prose of W.B. Yeats*, Vol. I, ed. John P. Frayne, Macmillan, 1975; Vol. II, ed. John P. Frayne & Colton Johnson, Macmillan, 1975

– *The Collected Letters of W.B. Yeats*, general editor John Kelly, Oxford University Press, 1986–. The first three volumes of the projected twelve or more are now in print

– *The Senate Speeches of W.B. Yeats*, ed. Donald R. Pearce, Faber & Faber, 1961

– *A Vision and Related Writings*, ed. A. Norman Jeffares, Arrow Books, 1990

– *Letters of W.B. Yeats*, ed. Allan Wade, Rupert Hart-Davis, 1954

Letters on Poetry from W.B. Yeats to Dorothy Wellesley, Oxford University Press, 1940

SOME CRITICAL STUDIES

The books listed here are selected as likely to help readers' understanding of Yeats's poetry.

C.M. Bowra, *The Heritage of Symbolism*, Macmillan, 1943
    A good survey of the **Symbolist** movement in Europe

Malcolm Brown, *The Politics of Irish Literature from Thomas Davis to W.B. Yeats*, Allen & Unwin, 1972
    A careful, balanced study

Peter Costello, *The Heart grown Brutal*, Gill & Macmillan, Dublin 1977
    Lively, provocative and well informed

Elizabeth Cullingford, *Yeats and Politics*, Macmillan, 1980

Denis Donoghue, *Yeats*, Collins, 1971
    A sensitive general study

Richard Ellmann, The Man and the Masks, Macmillan, 1949
    Makes good use of material unpublished before

– *The Identity of Yeats*, Faber & Faber, 1965
Explores the nature of Yeats's personality

Maud Gonne MacBride, *A Servant of the Queen*, Colin Smythe, 19xx
Maud Gonne's selective account of her life

Lady Augusta Gregory, *Seventy Years*, Colin Smythe, 1974
A good account of Yeats's friend and collaborator

T.R. Henn, *The Lonely Tower*, Methuen, 1965
Very good on Yeats and art

A. Norman Jeffares, *A New Commentary on the Poems of W.B. Yeats*, Macmillan, 1984
This gives the likely sources of poems and quotes relevant passages of Yeats's prose illuminating them

A. Norman Jeffares, *W.B. Yeats. Man and Poet*, Gill & Macmillan, 3rd edition, 1996

A. Norman Jeffares, ed., *Yeats, Sligo and Ireland*, Colin Smythe, 1980

A. Norman Jeffares, ed., *Yeats the European*, Colin Smythe, 1989

A. Norman Jeffares and A.S. Knowland, *A Commentary on the Collected Plays of W.B. Yeats*, Macmillan, 1975

A. Norman Jeffares and Anna MacBride White, eds, *The Gonne–Yeats Letters*, Hutchinson, 1992
This fills in many gaps in our knowledge of their relationship. Anna MacBride White is Maud Gonne's granddaughter

Peter Kuch, *Yeats and A.E.: the Antagonism that Unites Friends*, Colin Smythe, 1985
An excellent study analysing their complex relationship

Louis MacNeice, *The Poetry of W.B. Yeats*, Oxford University Press, 1941
Still a stimulating piece of criticism

Giorgio Melchiori, *The Whole Mystery of Art: Pattern into Poetry in the Work of W.B. Yeats*, Routledge, 1960
An intellectual analysis of Yeats's mental processes

Liam Miller, *The Noble Drama of W.B. Yeats*, Dolmen Press, 1977
A straightforward and discerning book

Virginia Moore, *The Unicorn*, Macmillan, 1954
An uneven book with some good insights

William M. Murphy, *Prodigal Father: the Life of John Butler Yeats (1839–1922)*, Cornell University Press, 1978
A book which conveys the nature of the Yeats household

Ann Saddlemyer and Colin Smythe, eds, *Lady Gregory Fifty Years After*, Colin Smythe, 1987
Contains a very good essay by John Kelly on the friendship of Yeats and Lady Gregory

Jon Stallworthy, *Between the Lines: Yeats's poetry in the Making*, Oxford University Press, 1963
A good account of Yeats's methods of writing

Donald Torchiana, *Yeats and Georgian Ireland*, Oxford University Press, 1966
A very useful book on the background of Yeats's interest in the eighteenth century

John Unterecker, *A Reader's Guide to W.B. Yeats*, Thames and Hudson, 1959

Helen Hennessy Vendler, *Yeats's Vision and the Later Plays*, Harvard University Press, 1963
A discriminating piece of criticism

G.J. Watson, *Irish Identity and the Literary Revival*, Croom Helm, 1979
A corrective to some transatlantic criticism

Robert Welch, *Irish Poetry from Moore to Yeats*, Colin Smythe, 1980
A good historical approach

F.A.C. Wilson, *W.B. Yeats and Tradition*, Gollancz, 1958
Stimulating if sometimes apt to offer theories as facts

Events	Author's life	Literary world
1845-9 The Great Famine in Ireland: 1 million die; 1.5 million emigrate		
1847 Ireland left to 'operation of natural causes'; death of Daniel O'Connell		**1847** William Carleton, *The Black Prophet*
		1852 Lady Augusta Gregory, leading figure in Irish Revival, born
		1856 George Bernard Shaw born
1858 Irish Republican Brotherhood founded; Fenian Brotherhood founded in America		
		1863 Ferguson, *Lays of Western Gael*
	1865 William Butler Yeats born, Dublin	
	1866 Yeats's sister Susan Mary (Lily) born, Sligo	
1867 Fenian rising in Ireland	**1867** Family moves to London	
	1871 John Butler (Jack) Yeats born	**1871** J.B. Synge born
	1872-4 Mrs Yeats and children in Sligo	
1874 First Impressionist exhibitions	**1874** Family moves to West London	
	1877-81 Yeats attends Godolphin School, Hammersmith, with holidays in Sligo	
1879 Threat of famine and evictions in Ireland		
1880 Charles Parnell elected leader of the Irish Party		**1880** Standish O'Grady, *History of Ireland: The Heroic Period*
	1881 Family moves to Dublin	

Events	Author's life	Literary world
	1881-3 Yeats attends High School, Dublin	
		1882 James Joyce born
	1884-6 Yeats at Metropolitan School of Art, Dublin	
	1885 Yeats attends first meeting of Dublin Hermetic Society	
1886 Home Rule Bill for Ireland defeated		
	1887 Family moves back to London; mother has two strokes; Yeats joins Theosophical Society	
	1888 *Fairy and Folk Tales of the Irish Peasantry*	**1888** T.S. Eliot born
	1889 *The Wanderings of Oisin; Crossways;* falls in love with Maud Gonne	
1890 Parnell cited in O'Shea divorce case; rejected by the Irish Party	**1890** Founds Rhymers Club; admitted into Order of the Golden Dawn	**1890** Frazer, *The Golden Bough*
1891 Death of Parnell	**1891** *Representative Irish Tales; John Sherman and Doya;* founds Irish Literary Society; turned down by Maud Gonne	
	1892 *Irish Fairy Tales; Countess Cathleen* first performed	**1892** Hyde, 'On the Necessity of De-Anglicising the Irish People'
1893 Foundation of Gaelic League	**1893** *The Celtic Twilight; The Rose;* meets Lady Gregory	**1893** Hyde, *Love Songs of Connacht;* Francis Thompson, *Poems*
	1894 *The Land of Heart's Desire*	
1896 Connolly founds Irish Socialist Republican Party	**1896** Affair with Olivia Shakespear	
		1898 Thomas Hardy, *Wessex Poems*

Events	Author's life	Literary world
	1899 Co-founds Irish Literary Theatre; *The Wind Among the Reeds*	
	1900 *The Shadowy Waters*	**1900** Death of Ernest Dowson, Symbolist poet
1901 Accession of Edward VII		
	1902 *Cathleen ni Houlihan*	**1902** Lady Gregory, *Cuchulain of Muirthemne*
1903 Irish Land Act leads to tenants purchasing land	**1903** Maud Gonne marries MacBride	
	1904 *In the Seven Woods*	**1904** Shaw, *John Bull's Other Island*
1905 Sinn Fein founded; Fauve exhibition, Paris	**1905** *Stories of Red Hanrahan*	
	1907 Visits Italy	**1907** Synge, *Playboy of the Western World*
	1908 *Collected Works;* visits Maud Gonne in Paris	
		1909 Synge dies
1910 Accession of George V	**1910** *The Green Helmet and Other Poems*	
	1911 Visits USA; meets Georgie Hyde Lees	**1911** Ezra Pound, *Canzoni;* Brooke, *Poems*
1912 Third Home Rule Bill; Ulster Volunteers, Irish Citizens Army and Irish National Volunteers founded		**1912** Marsh edits *Georgian Poetry*
	1913 *Poems written in Discouragement*	
1914 Outbreak of First World War	**1914** *Responsibilities*	**1914** James Joyce, *Dubliners;* George Moore, *Hail and Farewell*
1916 Leaders of Easter Rising shot		
	1917 Marries Georgie Hyde Lees; buys tower at Ballylee	**1917** Eliot, *Prufrock and Other Observations*
1918 War ends		**1918** Wilfred Owen dies

Events	Author's life	Literary world
1919 First meeting of Dail Eireann	**1919** Daughter Anne born; *The Wild Swans at Coole*	**1919** Siegfried Sassoon, *The War Poems*
1920 Ireland partitioned		
1921 Anglo-Irish Treaty	**1921** *Michael Robartes and the Dancer*	
1922 Civil War	**1922** *Seven Poems and a Fragment;* becomes Senator	**1922** Joyce, *Ulysses;* Eliot, *The Waste Land;* Edith Sitwell, *Façade*
	1923 Nobel Prize for Literature	
	1925 *A Vision*	
1927 O'Higgins, Minister in Irish Free State, assassinated	**1927** *October Blast*	
	1928 *The Tower*	**1928** Thomas Hardy dies
		1929 Robert Bridges, *Testament of Beauty*
1931 The Depression		**1931** Russell (AE), *The Vale and Other Poems*
	1932 *Words for Music Perhaps ...*	**1932** Lady Gregory dies
	1933 *The Winding Stair*	**1933** Stephen Spender, *Poems*
	1934 *Wheels and Butterflies*	**1934** Dylan Thomas, *Eighteen Poems*
	1935 *A Full Moon in March*	**1935** Louis Macniece, *Poems*
1936 Spanish Civil War, abdication of Edward VIII; Jarrow Hunger March		
	1938 *New Poems*	
1939 Second World War declared	**1939** **Death;** *Last Poems*	**1939** Seamus Heaney born

allegory an allegorical story exists as an autonomous narrative, but has another hidden second meaning

alliteration a sequence of repeated consonantal sounds in a stretch of language. The matching consonants are usually at the beginning of words or stressed syllables

assonance the correspondence, or near-correspondence, in the stressed vowel of two or more words

ballad a poem or song which tells a story in simple, colloquial language

Celtic Twilight originally the title of a collection of stories by Yeats (1893) expressing the mysticism of the Irish, their belief in fairies and spirits, it gave its name to the kind of literature produced by his imitators: romantic, sometimes vague, dreamy and wistful, and eventually became a generic phrase for the whole Irish revival in literature

consonance repeated arrangements of consonants, with a change in the vowel that separates them

couplet a pair of rhymed lines of any metre

elegy a poem of lamentation, concentrating on the death of a single person

genre a kind or type of literature

Georgian poetry usually refers to poets who wrote during the reign of George V (1910–36), including such poets as W.H. Davies, Walter de la Mare, Ralph Hodgson and Rupert Brooke; also Edward Thomas and Wilfred Owen

imagery/images in its narrowest sense an image is a word-picture, a description of some visible scene or object. More commonly, 'imagery' refers to the figurative language, such as metaphors and similes, in a piece of literature, or to words which refer to objects and qualities which appeal to the senses and feelings

Imagism a movement in poetry in England and America initiated by Ezra Pound and T.E. Hulme in about 1912. Its aims were: direct treatment of the 'thing' whether subjective or objective; to use absolutely no word that does not contribute to the presentation; and as regards rhythm, to compose in the sequence of the musical phrase, not in sequence of a metronome. Pound defined 'Image' as 'that which presents an intellectual and emotional complex in an instant of time'

irony in general terms, saying one thing while meaning another

lyric a poem, usually short, expressing in a personal manner the feelings and thoughts of an individual speaker (not necessarily those of the poet)

metaphor goes further than a comparison between two different things or ideas by fusing them together

metaphysical usually applied to a group of seventeenth-century poets, including Donne, Herbert and Vaughan and their abrasive colloquiality, their density and range of metaphorical associations and witty display of ingenious comparisons, conceits, paradoxes and puns

metre verse is distinguished from prose because it contains some linguistic element which is repeated, creating a sense of pattern. In English verse the commonest pattern is stress- or accent-based metre, which consists of the regular arrangement of strong stresses in a stretch of language

Neoplatonism system of philosophy based on Plato's ideas, especially modified by Plotinus and other new Platonists of the third to fifth centuries, whose work was revitalised during the Renaissance

octave a stanza of eight lines

ottava rima an eight-line iambic stanza, usually rhyming *abababcc*

persona originally referred to the mask used by actors in the Classical theatre, but which has come to mean, in literary terms, the point of view of a person who is clearly not the author, for the purpose of narration

quatrain a stanza of four lines

rhetoric the art of speaking and writing effectively so as to persuade an audience

rhyme chiming or matching sounds at the ends of lines of verse which create an audible sense of pattern

rhythm the variation of levels of stress accorded to the syllables. In verse the rhythm is more or less controlled and regular

sestet a stanza of six lines, or the last six lines of a Petrarchan sonnet

simile a figure of speech in which one thing is said to be like another and the comparison is made with the use of 'like' or 'as'

scansion the examination and analysis of the metre of a piece of verse

sonnet a lyric poem of fourteen lines of iambic pentameter rhymed and organised according to several intricate schemes. Petrarchan sonnets are divided in octave and sestet, rhymed *abbaabba ede cde* or *cdcecd*, while Shakespearean sonnets are divided into three quatrains and a couplet, rhymed *abab bcbc cdcd ee*

sprezzatura (Italian: careless rapture or improvisation) nonchalant grace and ease

stanza a unit of several lines of verse

stream of consciousness the flow of consciousness in a character's mind – memory, sense perceptions, feelings, intuitions, thoughts, in relation to the stream of experience as it passes by, often randomly – without intervention by the author

symbol something that represents something else (often an abstract quality), by analogy or allusion

Symbolist Movement a movement originating in the nineteenth century in France with Baudelaire, Rimbaud, Verlaine, Mallarmé and Valéry, whose poetry exploited the mysterious suggestiveness of private symbols. They concentrated on achieving a musical quality in their verse and believed that through blurring the senses and mixing images they depicted a higher reality. Yeats, Pound and Eliot were deeply influenced by the French movement

AUTHOR OF THIS NOTE

When editing his school magazine in 1937 A. Norman Jeffares persuaded Yeats (an old boy of the Erasmus Smith High School, Dublin) to contribute a new poem to it. He has written extensively on the poet's life and work, his books including *Yeats: Man and Poet* (3rd edn 1996), *A New Commentary on the Poems of Yeats* (2nd edn 1984), *Yeats: A New Biography* (1988) and *Yeats's Poems* (3rd edn 1996). He has also written and edited books on Irish, English, American and Commonwealth authors, and has held academic posts in Ireland, Holland, Scotland, Australia and England.